PERCEPTION MASTERY

SEVEN SIMPLE STEPS TO LASTING CHANGE

BECA LEWIS

PERCEPTION PUBLISHING

ISBN: 978-1-7357843-4-2

Copyright ©2021 by Beca Lewis
All rights reserved.

Perception Mastery first Copyright©2021. All rights reserved. No part of this book may be reproduced or transmitted in any form or by any means, electronic or mechanical, including photocopying, recording, or by any information storage and retrieval system, without written permission from the author, except for the inclusion of brief quotations in a review as permitted by U.S. copyright law.

WHAT OTHERS SAY ...

Beca's *Perception Mastery* book is a gold mine of spiritual wisdom and invaluable methods to help you shift into higher levels of self-awareness. Beca designed this book to help you turn inward so that you can examine limiting beliefs in all areas of your life and shift your thinking to create and live your best life.

I enjoyed this book and all of Beca's books in *The Shift Series* because they are grounded in practical spirituality. Beca teaches effective, simple methods that have helped me shift my thinking and energetics to better align with the flow of universal abundance and create my life through my conscious intentions. We all have the ability to turn inward.

We have a choice in every moment, and when we slow down to listen to our soul, magic truly happens. If you are curious and willing, then read this book. —Tracy Wright Corvo

***

Let's face it. Humans tend to be creatures of habit. Why wouldn't we be, since we spend so much time dwelling on habits? And we know that what we focus on is pretty much what we get, right? That's what the *Perception Mastery* book is all about. Perception and habits. Beca teaches us that "Perception produces reality, and what we perceive as reality magnifies."

If that is true, and I maintain that it is, the best thing we can do is perceive the best reality we can possibly imagine! And if habits are so ingrained in us, why not choose the best ones we can?

So, by shifting to the highest understanding we can imagine now by following simple principles and using some pretty nifty tools Beca teaches, not only are we learning to live our best lives, but by learning for ourselves, we are extending that benefit to the world. —Jet Tucker

Contents

Introduction	VIII
Find A Friend	X
1. Why Become A Perception Master	1
The Seven Steps To Shift	6
2. Step One: Be Willing	7
3. Step Two: Become Aware	23
4. Step Three: Understand Signs And Symbols	39
5. Step Four: Perception Rules	64
6. Step Five: Choose Spiritual Perception	91
7. Step Six: Walk As One	110
8. Step Seven: Celebrate With Gratitude	124
Acknowledgments	139
About Beca	140

Also By Beca

INTRODUCTION

Reading is seeing by proxy. — Herbert Spencer

All the books in *The Shift Series* are the "children" of the first book in the series, *Living In Grace: The Shift To Spiritual Perception*. Each book addresses an idea brought forth in *Living In Grace* and expands upon it.

Like all the books in *The Shift Series*, *Perception Mastery* is a self-help book based on spiritual principles designed to support your personal spiritual practice.

Perception Mastery focuses directly on the rules of perception, which underlies all the concepts found in *Living In Grace*. Perhaps it should have been the first offshoot? Or maybe I needed to teach and coach for many years to understand how to set out the ideas more clearly and practically, which is why this book took so long to write.

It doesn't matter in what order you read *The Shift Series*. Following your internal guidance, you will find the one that will help you the most where you are in life.

However, each book has an intent, or more accurately, I have an intent for each book.

For *Perception Mastery*, it is to provide you, the reader, with tools that will:

- Give you a clearer understanding of your unique spiritual expression and how to live it.

- Help you master the experience of joy under all circumstances.

- Increase your ability to ask for and accept the overflowing abundance of Life's gifts.

- And as a result, experience a recognizable shift towards the life you want to live.

I know not every question or possibility is addressed in this book, but it is a sound foundation to build upon. Use it as a guide, a blueprint to practice mastering perception.

I trust that you have the inner wisdom and understanding to find what you need within these pages and will use it to expand your awareness of infinite possibilities for yourself and others.

Thank you for walking this spiritual path with me. — Beca!

Sometimes the shortest distance between two points is a winding path walked arm in arm. — Robert Brault

FIND A FRIEND

*A man is known by the company his mind keeps. —
Thomas Bailey Aldrich*

To make this book even more fun and practical, perhaps you would like to do the steps with a friend or two because often it is helpful to do spiritual work within a community—however, not just any community, a community of like-minded souls.

Always choose your community of friends and confidants carefully. Make sure you all have each other's best interests in mind.

Not sure how to know if they are the right fit for you?

Ask yourself if you are a better person because you are together? Are you both kinder, more open, more confident, more joyful, more inclusive, and more supportive of every living thing? Then you are on the right track.

Don't know anyone who does this for you yet? You will because like-minded souls find each other when the time is right. In the meantime, read and do these steps yourself, knowing you are not really alone.

If you need help, let me know. There might be a group going on that you can join, or I could be teaching a live class just as you begin this. You can find me at becalewis.com.

Take this time for deep thinking and the chance to rejuvenate your life. Don't wait. Get started.

Things will shift to bring you what you need and want if you are faithful to the practice and yourself. It always begins within. And with faith.

Not sure you have faith? You do. Or you wouldn't have opened this book. That's enough faith right there.

Note: If you would like to use a workbook with this book, you can find one for free at Perceptionu.com.

1

WHY BECOME A PERCEPTION MASTER

If life had a second edition, how I would correct the proofs. — John Clare

Perception is reality. How many times have we all said these words and maybe even believed them?

But are they true? And if they are, does it matter?

Yes, they are, and yes, it does. But too often, we misinterpret the words when we don't realize that we are the producers of our perception.

As perception masters, we learn to shift the reality we perceive rather than perceiving a reality presented to us.

Contrary to what we might wish to be true, there is only one thing we can actually "control." One thing only. Our perception, and therefore our reaction, and response, to people, places, things, and events.

Isn't that fantastic? Rather than trying to control everything, all we need to do is shift our perception?

As Mary Baker Eddy said, "It's not what you see, but how you see it." Or, as Henry David Thoreau said, "It's not what you look at that matters, it's what you see."

And when we learn how to see with the eyes of perception masters or prophets, like Buddha, Elias, Christ Jesus, or Mohammad, we will experience an entirely different world. Not because we made it change, but because we see and experience it as it already is. Perfect. Eternal. Glorious.

If this appeals to you, come with me on this journey as we shift our perceptions together. Because until we can fully rise above the perception that we are human, or even spiritual beings having a human experience, we will constantly be called upon to shift our perception, so we might as well become masters of it.

Will this perception shifting change anything? Absolutely. Because yes, *what we perceive to be reality magnifies*. So since (our) perception is (our) reality, let's shift our perception to the most glorious, loving, unlimited view of existence that we can muster up. As we get better at it, so will the world that we view.

Want to change the world? Start within. Start with perception, yours.

Be a shifter. Be a perception shifter. Be a perception master. Be a shift master. Then get out of the way and observe what is really going on. It's better than you think.

So let's hop to it and get this party started!

One more thing: Do these steps in your own timing.

When I teach this class, we do one step a week. In this book, Molly, our guide, is doing one every few days.

Take these steps faster, slower, whatever works for you. In fact, once you know them, you could take yourself through them within minutes. No matter which way you choose, the important thing is to do them.

And expect results. Oh, and have fun. Why not? It's a perception, after all.

MEET MOLLY

The landscape belongs to the man who looks at it. — Ralph Waldo Emerson

Molly is a made-up person. However, she became pretty real to me as I wrote this book. I think that's because she is a composite of all of us, and I recognized myself in her. As I think you will too.

Molly will work through each step of this book and share what she learns, which will help explain how each step of this process might play out in your life. Of course, not exactly.

But if we peek at what she thinks as she perfects her perception skills, it should help explain how to use the concepts and steps in real-life situations.

In a class, we talk about what we learn together, and that sharing helps remind us not only that we can do it, but we are not alone. So instead of classmates, we have Molly, a composite of all of us at different times in our lives. Although we are all beautifully diverse expressions of the Divine, we have much in common.

If you have a trusted friend doing this book with you, talk about what you learn together. You'll be pleasantly surprised to discover how much that helps.

No matter what, Molly's experience should help your experience. That's my intent anyway.

THE SEVEN STEPS TO SHIFT

2

STEP ONE: BE WILLING

He who would may reach the utmost height, but he must be eager to learn. — Buddha

This first step—Be Willing—is so important it could take up the entire book. And even though all the other steps might not need to be in the order that I present them, this one always must come first. All the time. Every time.

Because unless we are willing for something to change or shift, or become better. it can't.

Why? Because we are the ones holding the perception of a reality as a truth for us. And even though the entire universe could have changed, we won't notice unless we are willing to see the change.

Or we will experience the change through our personal paradigm filter, which means it will be a skewed view.

If you were wearing a pair of blue glasses, and I tried to tell you that the world is not only blue but beautiful shades of many colors, if you are not willing to take off the glasses, then the world will forever be only blue to you.

That nothing can happen unless we are willing is so clear that it's incredible how often we ignore it. And yet, we can see for ourselves that we can't, won't, don't, do anything unless we are willing to do it.

There is no way around this first step. But being willing cannot be forced on anyone or faked. It has to be voluntary, for both us and for those we wish were willing.

This book will help you open up the space for being willing. It will help you find the thoughts, ideas, and paradigms you have either not noticed, or noticed and didn't know how to change, so that you can either consciously choose to keep them or be willing to let them go.

Yes, we do things every day that we don't want to do. To do them, a part of us was willing. Discovering that reason will help us do things we don't do, even though we want to.

Imagine what it would be like to be consciously aware of whether or not we are willing. Imagine what it would be like if we realized we weren't willing to do something, and why we aren't willing, accept that we aren't willing, and be able to say no and mean it.

Or imagine what it would be like to be entirely in the willing mode to do what we want and experience the joy of the flow it would produce.

Learning how to recognize our unwillingness and improve our willingness is a practice. Although a straightforward concept, it involves a depth of awareness that most of us don't possess most of the time.

However, we can become skilled in this practice, and that's what we will do together.

Before we begin, why not prove this concept of willingness for yourself?

And even though, as in all things, we must begin within to shift our perception, let's start our discovery by looking outside ourselves and into our life.

Everyone has someone in their life that doesn't do what we want them to do. In fact, isn't a large part of life about trying to convince others to do something? Get our children to pick up their toys, be polite, don't slurp your food, hang out with the right people, pick the right school, fall in love with the right person.

What about what we want from our life partners, parents, our work colleagues? If they would only listen to us, everything would be so much better. Or on a broader scale. Politicians. What's wrong with them, anyway? Why don't they do want we want them to do? Why are they swayed by things we know are the wrong things?

How do we convince them? Some of us are more skilled at this than others, and all of us are terrible at it at times. And you know why? Because we can't change someone's mind, including our own, unless they, and we, are willing.

That's it. If someone is not willing, we have two choices.

1. We can stop trying to make happen what will never happen and is only causing us to beat our heads against a wall, hurting ourselves and others in the process.

2. Or we have to make space for them to become willing. And if they are not, let it go.

Make space. That is not the way we think about changing things. We usually push into change.

Instead, we will practice stepping back and making space for change.

And that begins where it must, within ourselves.

Are you willing to do that? Is there anything in your life that is causing you enough pain and frustration that you can say, *"Okay, I am willing. Nothing else has worked. Yes, I am willing."*

Isn't this the concept of organizations like AA? Nothing will change until the person suffers enough to be willing. Hits bottom.

But we don't have to get to suffering for this to work. You could suffer if you want to. Go ahead, go for it. But I'm tired of suffering—both my own and others. I would prefer that we all learn by following the light and angel ideas rather than experience suffering.

I, and you, may not be able to avoid some of this suffering. It will appear to come from the outside. Something outside our control. 2020 was the perfect example of this. All of us suffered—some more than others.

What we were willing to do with it made the difference and will make a difference as we move forward. It was the perfect lens for us to use to study our willingness. Our willingness to change. Our willingness to not react. Our willingness to help others.

So our first step in this seven-step shift of perception is to be willing, and the first thing we need to do to become artists at willingness is to discover what we are willing and unwilling to do and then decide what to do about it.

A cautionary note. The willingness I am talking about is not about human willpower. It's not about making something happen or creating it. That's not the willing meant here. This is a willingness for letting go and experiencing the intelligent, loving, creative force that is all around us, providing for us in every moment.

You don't have to believe this. You just have to be willing to find out if it is true.

That's the big picture.

The everyday picture is a little simpler. Are we willing to live differently, or get along with someone we don't like, or learn a new technology?

Are we willing to let it be okay that other people, even those we love, are not willing? Not willing to do what we want for them or think is best for them. Are we willing to let them be who and what they want to be?

In this way, we can still love them, listen, and understand, which may provide a safe space for them to be willing. Even so, we have to be willing that they might never get there.

A key point.

Often it is good not to be willing. I am not willing to intentionally hurt another or myself. I am not willing to sit on a hot stove. I am not willing to listen to people who only mean harm.

So, understanding our boundaries is a process of being willing, and that's a good thing.

Remember, we are not changing our human minds. We are releasing them so that we can see more. We are taking off those blue glasses. Ready! Go!

THE TWO WORD KEY TO EVERYTHING

Sooner or later everyone sits down to a banquet of consequences.
— Robert Louis Stevenson

How many times have you tried to change someone, or even yourself, and failed miserably?

Without knowing a single thing about what happened or what you were trying to do, I know why it probably didn't work as well as you wanted it to.

One day, I decided I wanted to stop getting in my way. I wasn't doing anything overt. However, I could feel myself not letting things happen. Very subtle. But it was becoming quite annoying. I wanted to experience more of what we all know, that the universe moves towards us, and the Infinite loves to provide us with what we want and desire.

I asked myself, "If that's true, why does everything stay about the same?" After all, we live in an ever-expanding universe filled with more riches than we can ever imagine. Why don't all of us consistently experience an overabundance of wealth in all its forms?

The answer is simple. The solution is also simple, but not easy.

PERCEPTION MASTERY

We have to break the habit of consciously and unconsciously saying no to what is being offered. We have to stop the habit of walking away from the open hand, bearing gifts.

Why do we do this? Perhaps we think we're not worthy. Or we believe we can do it ourselves, thank you very much. Or we are self-contained. Or we are afraid that having what we want will bring us responsibilities that we don't think we can handle. Or we are trapped in our habits.

For sure, our perceptions have made us prisoners of what we believe.

We allow enough abundance into our lives to keep us comfortable in whatever manner we expect or are used to. But against more than that, we erect a barrier. Yes, invisible most of the time, but still a barrier.

When I am paying attention, I can feel the barriers I've put up. Observing my habits, I realize I have lots of them hanging out in the tiny crevices of my life, ready to be called into action if I should need them. They willingly spring into action if there is too much supply of wealth in my life.

So I took to heart, once again—because I, like you, have done this countless times in my life—the first step of any shift. I decided to be willing. Really willing. Consciously willing. Willing to say yes. Willing to break old habits.

It's easy to say we are willing. But are we?

Inside, unconsciously, are we shutting down our energy? Are we blocking help? Are we saying, "that's too much for me to handle?"

To change anything at all, from life to light bulbs, we have to be willing. And when we are willing—well, stand back because things will flow.

The universe moves towards us and pools at our feet, providing what we need long before asking for it. We stand on the abundant earth that has been given to us. We walk through its air, drink its water, glory in its beauty. Can not the Intelligence that provides all this provide for its loved ones? It can. It does. Say yes.

Say yes to what Life wants to give you.

Be willing to do what it takes to receive it. Be willing to ask for help. Be willing to step forward into your gifts. The gift always contains a way to use it. Would an intelligent divine Mind design Life any other way?

Be willing is the key to what works and what doesn't. We can't help anyone if they are not willing, including ourselves. It's the first step to making any shift or change in our lives. Be willing. Everything flows from that one point.

My dance teacher at UCLA used to say, "Expand, take up space." It's the same thing. Be willing to be who you are, and surrender to abundance.

Be willing—the two-word key to everything.

BE A SHIFTER

By giving up the need to know, we can begin to know in a whole new way. — Shinzen Young

As you know, in the fantasy world, a shifter is someone who can be many things. Some of them are dragons (I have a dragon or two in my fantasy books). Others can be anything at all, from a bird to a fish to a different being altogether. My favorite fantasy shifter is Odo from Deep Space Nine.

However, to be a shifter in our world, we have to become perception masters. And to do that, we must first be willing to accept that each of us contains within our essence all that we need—as does the person we love the most and the person we like the least.

We all have unlimited possibilities to shift to who we want to be, which is who we were designed to be.

To become more willing, sometimes it helps to imagine ourselves as trees, the sky, a light beam, or—the list is endless. If you have read my *Imagination Mastery* book, you are already doing this kind of thing. If not, this is an excellent time to begin.

What good does it do? It shifts us out of the limited human view of ourselves, which is minuscule compared to who we truly are, and imagination expands that paradigm.

Keep that in mind as we go forward. And remember, although you are becoming a perception master for yourself, it will help others too. As Michael Jackson said, start with the man in the mirror.

> *I'm gonna make a change*
> *For once in my life*
> *It's gonna feel real good*
> *Gonna make a difference*
> *Gonna make it right*

> *No message could have been any clearer*
> *If you want to make the world a better place*
> *Take a look at yourself and then make the change*
> — Michael Jackson, *Man In The Mirror*

Practical Willing

Whenever two people meet, there are really six people present. There is each man as he sees himself, each man as the other person sees him, and each man as he really is. — William James

Let's prime your pump of self-discovery.

Here are questions you can ask yourself:

1. Am I willing to be aware of the abundance that is already present—in all its forms?

- Am I willing to let go of the beliefs that bind me to a sense of lack?

- Am I willing to live as my unique spiritual blessing?

- Am I willing to feel worthy?

- Am I willing to let go, willing to do what is asked of me, willing to be open, willing to set boundaries, willing to have no desires, willing to have everything, willing to follow inspiration, willing to wake up, willing to stop hurting, willing to be happy, willing not to be liked, willing to be loved, willing to let Truth be my only guide?

All these are examples of being willing. I'm sure you can think of many more.

Asking yourself these questions doesn't mean that you know how to experience these things right now. Or even that you believe they are possible. All that is important is the willingness to find out for yourself.

And remember, knowing that you are not willing to do some things is essential too. There is no judgment on any of this. Otherwise, we will never get to the core truth of what you want and who you are.

Don't judge. Observe. You are not your personality or what claims to be your human self. So be kind to yourself. It's doing its best. Instead, marvel at what you learn instead of judging it.

Tying It Together: Practical Willing

Ready? Willing? You are definitely able. So let's go. Write out your responses to these statements. Don't worry about what you are writing. You can clean it up later, but it's not necessary.

- I am willing to do these things:

- I am not willing to do these things:

- I am willing to take action on this:

Once again, don't try to change any of this. Just notice. Don't judge if it is either good or bad. Just write it down.

Say to yourself: *I am willing to shift. I am a shifter. I am a Perception Master!*

MOLLY AND BEING WILLING

The one who is truly wise sees the consequences of his actions. — Babylonian Talmud

Molly's friend Sally gave her the book *Perception Mastery* and suggested she read it. Molly said thanks. and then put the book away, thinking that the last thing she needed to read was a woo-woo book about shifting perception.

She had some genuine issues to deal with, and no amount of perception blah-blah would fix it. Besides, having the time and bandwidth for learning new things was for young people, not for people like her.

Molly couldn't decide if her problems were too big or too small to do anything about them. She should be grateful. She had a place to live, a husband, grown kids, even the makings of a garden.

Sure, she felt overworked and unappreciated, but didn't everyone? She didn't like her job, but they needed the money. And Molly realized that if she was going to be honest with herself, she also didn't enjoy being stuck in the house all day. So the job gave her a place to go.

The year of working from home and not going to the office almost made her crazy. Although Molly was grateful she kept her job when others lost theirs, she was bored. Still, it was a job.

The more Molly allowed herself to think about it, the more she believed it would be wrong to want more. She had work. They had money to buy groceries. Her children called once in a while. Her husband wasn't mean, and sometimes he did things to help around the house. What were her problems, anyway?

However, one day, while dusting, she ran across the book again. Flipping through the pages, Molly noticed that there were steps to being a perception master, whatever that was.

Still not understanding why she needed to shift her perception for anything to happen, she decided it couldn't hurt.

It was only later that she realized that choice was the point of the first step. She had become willing just a tiny bit. Enough to read the book and try out the exercises.

What Molly discovered as she did the exercises both shocked her and made her mad. Who she was mad at, she wasn't sure. But as her list grew of what she was not willing to do, she was astonished.

It was harder for her to make a list of what she was willing to do. Then she realized that her life mirrored back to her what she had been and was willing to do.

It was simple things, like shopping for groceries every day, dusting the house, doing a job that bored her. She was also willing to ignore the state of the house and garden. She was willing to wear clothes that didn't fit her and listen to news that depressed her.

Once she got started, Molly couldn't stop. Both lists grew. She tried not to judge them. She had to ask herself every day if she was willing only to notice, not judge. Sometimes she was. Often she wasn't.

Finally, she asked herself the question she might have asked at first. *Was she willing to be happy?*

When she realized her answer was no, she sat down on the bedroom floor and cried. How could she not be willing to be happy?

And then she realized she cried because she did want to be happy. Of course, she did. That meant she was willing. It was a revelation, and with that conscious choice to be willing to be happy, something changed for Molly.

If this was what perception mastery was about, she wanted more of it. She was willing.

3

STEP TWO: BECOME AWARE

Nothing remains as it was. If you know this, you can begin again, with pure joy in the uprooting. — Judith Minty

I know we would all like to think that we are aware, but you know that most of the time we are not. How could we be? If we were aware of all that is happening at all times, we probably couldn't function.

To enable us to live in the swarm of information that is our world, we have selective awareness, which is good. It keeps us focused. Our brains filter out what is unnecessary.

The problem is, if we aren't constantly checking, we get stuck in the paradigm we've created. Unless we actively choose to become aware of something other than what we currently know and believe, we stay stuck in an unyielding loop.

To experience the life we want to live, we must constantly be willing to see differently—to shift our perception. And to do that, we must become aware of what constitutes our current life and belief system.

Awareness is vital to our well-being because a lack of awareness keeps us at one end of a point of view in a distorted, conditioned mind, which is out of balance and at odds with the other end.

To release ourselves from the paradigms and belief systems that may have kept us safe at one point but now stop our progress, we have to be willing to become aware of our current physical, emotional, and mental states to uncover hidden thoughts and habits.

You will notice, as we walk this perception-shifting path together, that all these steps intertwine. Perception mastery is not a straight line. It curves and spirals, rises and falls.

However, these steps do have an obvious order. Take these first two. If we are going to be willing, we have to be aware of what we are willing to do or not do.

As we do this work, it's essential to remember that we all express our true spiritual nature differently. One is not better than another, just as one color in nature is not better than another. Contrary to what many of us have been taught to believe, we are not in competition with each other. Just as in all nature, cooperation is our natural state.

Yes, we all have different preferences and different desires, but they are designed to blend together, to live in harmony with each other. Therefore, it is essential that we become aware of our actual preferences and desires, not what we think they are or were told they are.

Yes, we are allowed to make choices that benefit us. Not only allowed. It is necessary. We can choose for ourselves, not blindly following previously set paradigms and perceptions. As perception masters, we make mindful, conscious choices.

As in all things in life, we practice if we want to become skilled at something. Now, as we practice being willing, we add in the skill of becoming aware. As we do so, we discover that there are things we should not be willing to do. Or things that others do we should not be willing to let happen.

So besides being willing to do, we also have to be willing not to do.

But how aware are you of what you are not willing to do?

"Beca," you might say. "You have lost your mind. I am not willing to do lots of things, and I am perfectly well aware of them."

Hum. Are you? Are we? And do you know the underlying reason you are not willing?

Because we all do things we tell ourselves that we are not willing to do, but we do anyway. All. The. Time.

And you know that we all are unwilling to do things we know we "should" be willing to do.

So what are we missing?

The why of it.

Why are you willing? Why are you not willing? What is the "voice in your head" telling you about your choices that keep you from moving forward or letting go?

In the practical awareness section, you'll be doing something very simple but extremely powerful. It's a perception tool I call "I Choose sheets."

If you have done them before-—since this is one tool I always talk about—welcome back. If not, don't worry. They are easy to understand. I'll tell you how to use them in the Practical Awareness section.

Stick with me here for a second as we talk about what this tool can do for you. Using an I Choose sheet not only begins the process of becoming aware but also grounds it into action.

When we become aware of what stops us from doing what we think we want to do, one of three things will happen:

1. Either… Having all the blocks removed, we are energized, excited, and are taking action steps towards what we are willing to do,

2. Or—nothing happens. At all. This is when you grab your handy paper and pen and start another I Choose sheet based on what you have learned. Or you could continue the one you are working on. Either way, keep going until the hidden block reveals its sneaky little self, releasing you from its hold,

3. Or—you discover, perhaps to your surprise, that you don't want to do it. Maybe you don't have the time, and you realize that something else is more important. Or it was something you used to want to do, but that desire belonged to a different you. One from a different time and place. Or it was something that others have told you one way or another that you wanted it.

Pausing here.

Our entire culture is designed to make us want or need something unnecessary. Buy this. Think that. Do it this way.

Becoming aware of our willingness and why we are willing—or not—is a critical step on our perception shifting path.

But sometimes, we don't pause long enough to listen.

I made that mistake as I was writing this book. I saw something. It spoke my language. It had a deadline. It had a bargain price. I bought it. Then I read more and realized they were selling fear. I hadn't noticed that. Two minutes after buying it, I canceled it. I heard my internal voice and listened to it.

Yes, it was a pain to cancel. But I was willing to do it, anyway.

We all make mistakes. But we'll make fewer ones, correct them more quickly, and learn what we need to know from them when we are willing to become aware.

Discovering that you don't want something you thought you did is time for a celebration. You've made space. You have given yourself a gift of time in your life. Now you have room for something with a better or a more current why.

Become aware of your choices. And be willing to choose it and see if it is still what you want.

Yes, this is an ongoing process. That's life for you! We might as well get to living it and celebrate the adventure.

Choose Consciously

I choose, therefore I am. — Amit Goswami

Did you know there's a voice in your head constantly telling you why you can't do something? This voice is called many things: the monkey voice, the ego, the shadow—whatever you call it, it's imperative to know and understand one thing. That voice is not your voice. I know it sounds like you, and it says things you think you might say to yourself, but it's not.

So, why is it there?

That's like asking why do we believe we are human. Who knows? At this point, it's all someone's story, believe them or not, it doesn't change anything.

Here's what we do know and does change things. The voice in our head runs the paradigm we think we must live within, and unless we know what it is saying to us, we are stuck in its prison. It drives the car we call our life. It has us choosing things we may or may not want anymore, or perhaps never wanted.

However, we do have free will, so let's put that freedom to work.

Let's find out what that voice is saying and then replace it with what we consciously choose. Being willing, becoming aware, and consciously choosing breaks open our current paradigm. It shifts our perception. And as a result, the world we experience shifts to match our new perception.

Remember, perception is reality. "What we perceive to be reality magnifies."

Therefore, since we can make conscious choices, let's shift our perception to the best version of what I call big R Reality we can get to right now. Which for me, and perhaps for you, is a gloriously Loving One Intelligent Reality because that's the one I want to experience.

Now that we know what we would consciously choose, let's do an I Choose sheet. Doing this is so simple it might seem ineffective. However, I promise you it works if you do it.

Here we go:

Get out a tablet of paper and a pen. Notice I didn't say get your computer. I love writing on my computer. But I Choose sheets work much better when they are handwritten. Besides, when you finish with one, you can burn it. Very satisfying.

Begin by stating what you want as a choice.

How do you know what you want? Remember the question you answered at the top of this chapter? What are you willing to do? Choose that.

After that, there are just two steps to learn.

- First, pause, listen for the voice in your head telling you why you can't have it or why it won't work.

I guarantee you that the voice is there. Don't worry. It can't hurt to hear it now. In fact, you want to listen to what it's been telling you all along, and you have been accepting as true.

Once you hear that voice telling you why you can't have what you are willing to do, don't write what that voice says. Please don't give it any power by agreeing with it.

- Next, choose and write the opposite of what it's saying. I call this "face and replace."

Face what it says, and replace it with what you consciously choose.

Let's head over to see how Molly does an I Choose sheet so you can see how it works.

Molly and Becoming Aware

The world is changed not by the self-regarding, but by men and women prepared to make fools of themselves. — P. D. James

Molly decided that the one thing she was willing to do was to be happy. And she was ready to take action towards that intent.

Choosing happiness was more complex than she thought it would be. Did she have a right to be happy? What was happy, anyway? But she knew that the point of this practice was to find answers to questions like this. That she was willing was a big step forward.

As for what Molly thought she wanted, and now realized that she was unwilling to do, was the idea that she would someday have a small farm with lots of animals.

That was a dream she had as a child. Now she realized she was not willing to do the work to pursue it. She could barely muster up the desire to keep a garden alive. It was a relief to let that idea go and focus on doing what made her happy now.

Molly discovered something else that she realized was important. Although she had a few projects she had been planning to do in the next month, Molly realized that if she wanted to become a perception master and discover what made her happy, she needed to put the projects aside for a few weeks and do this work first.

Molly hoped that by practicing the seven steps, she would find a better way to do the projects, or perhaps she would discover they weren't necessary. Either way, she accepted that she only had so much time, and instead of being upset about that, Molly chose to take the time to understand how to shift her perception.

Molly knew it was a skill that would come in handy for almost anything. If, in the process, she discovered more about her true spiritual nature, well, that would be glorious. If it only made her life a bit better, and she felt a little happier, it would be worth it.

Here's the beginning of Molly's I Choose sheet. Follow this format precisely for yourself. Your voice may say entirely different things. It knows you well.

Notice that often the voice repeats itself. Stay strong. Deny what it says. It will give up.

You choose. You listen (face). And choose again (replace).
- Molly writes: I choose to be happy.

She hears the voice say: "You don't know how to be happy."
- Molly writes: I choose to know how to be happy.

She hears the voice say: "No one is happy."
- Molly writes: I choose to be happy.

She hears the voice say: "You have no right to be happy."
- Molly writes: I choose to know that I do have a right

PERCEPTION MASTERY

to be happy.

She hears the voice say: "You don't know what happiness is."
- Molly writes: I choose to understand what makes me happy.

She hears the voice say: "People will be mad if you are happy."
- Molly writes: I choose to have people around me who love that I am happy,

She hears the voice say: "The world is a sad, lonely, and frightening place."
- Molly writes: I choose to experience a happy world, filled with friends, and a safe place to thrive.

She hears the voice say: "You have no friends."
- Molly writes: I choose to have friends.

She hears the voice say: "Your husband doesn't want you to change."
- Molly writes: I choose to know my husband wants me to be happy.

Okay—you get the idea. You can see that Molly could go on with this I Choose sheet for many, many pages. That's a good thing. We all have multiple hidden beliefs that run our life.

Being aware of them, choosing consciously to face and replace them, works so well it may feel like magic. And yet, it can be scary. Our human self, ego, is going to fade away, and it doesn't want to. It's okay to be afraid. But don't let that fear stop you. It's the path towards freedom from the voice running your life.

Feel the fear, and do it anyway.

Molly keeps on writing for days. Watching the twists and turns of where this takes her becomes more exciting than worrying about what will happen. And to her surprise and delight, Molly realizes happiness has been there all along, just waiting for her to clear out the clutter of old beliefs and perceptions.

Molly keeps writing more I Choose sheets before moving on to the next step, Understanding Signs and Symbols.

Here are Molly's answers to the Practical Becoming Aware questions.

*What did you become most aware of?
That I have a hard time knowing what I want.
*What did you choose to be willing to do?
I chose to be willing to be open to doing a different kind of work.
*Why?
Because I am tired of being confused and unhappy about it.
*What action did you take to do it?
I am making a list of things I like to do.
*What are you not willing to do?
Complain about my work.
*Why?

Because complaining makes nothing better and distracts me from happiness.

*What action did you take to stop doing it?
I stopped that voice as soon as I heard the complaining.

PRACTICAL AWARENESS

Live the actual moment. Only this moment is life. — Thich Nhat Hanh

Before we move deeper into awareness, look back at your willingness answers in the last chapter.

These don't have to be long answers—just a note to yourself is sufficient.

Now, narrow down your answers to the one you want to focus on today.

What one thing are you willing to do and take action on?

This answer will be the basis for your first I Choose sheet.

But first, let's do a Becoming Aware exercise. This exercise can be very enlightening, so try it. Make notes to yourself about what you find.

Notice:

What's in your house: In a drawer. In a closet.
What someone is saying.

What you do with your time.
What you don't do with your time.
How you think about something.
How you do something.
What you listen to.
What you believe.

Look where you normally don't look. Listen where you normally don't listen.

Make a list of what you most want to become aware of during this exercise.

Ask yourself why.

And, as always, avoid judgment, shaming, and regret. That was then. This is now. Let's get on with it without the unneeded and unnecessary baggage that no Loving Creator would ever ask us to carry.

Get the lesson. Say thanks. Move on.

And, here's an exciting part! You will, I promise, discover that you already have many things that you think you want. Already present. Perhaps wrapped in a package that you, until this moment, didn't recognize.

Don't worry if you haven't experienced this yet. We'll do more exercises later in this book to help open your awareness even more to what is already present.

Here's the most fantastic thing. No matter how much abundance, love, grace, opportunities, etc., you have now, there is always more waiting to be seen when you are ready.

And now that you have a few ideas to work with, you can consciously choose and discover a why or two.

Tying It Together: Becoming Aware

(Check back to see how Molly answered these questions if you need to prime the pump.)

Write the answers to these questions:
- What did you become most aware of?

- What did you choose to be willing to do? Why?

- What action did you take to do it?

- What are you not willing to do? Why?

- What action did you take to stop doing it?

Make an I Choose sheet about at least one of these questions. We'll learn more about I Choose sheets later in this book and this way you'll have some to use when we get there.

4

STEP THREE: UNDERSTAND SIGNS AND SYMBOLS

Matter is matter only to the material state of consciousness, but once we rise to a mental state of consciousness, matter is not matter, but mind. — Joel S. Goldsmith

Why this step? Because the outside, visible world is the projection of the internal and nonvisible inner world of our point of view and state of mind. We learn either the essence of the Truth they are revealing or the lie they are telling through signs and symbols.

They are the mirror that reflects back to us what we believe to be true. Then we can adjust our perception to clean up the view, just as we would adjust our clothes or hair or check our teeth in the bathroom mirror. Doing so changes the reflection because we have changed ourselves.

Obviously, we must know how to discern the difference between "good" and "bad" signs because signs and symbols make up every part of life—from traffic to nature.

Understanding the difference between signs and symbols of what is True and the reversal of what is True is crucial.

Often we wait for something to "tell" us what to do. We ask for a sign to direct us. We don't realize that in doing so, we still can only see what we have become willing to see based on our current paradigm.

I used to choose to do things I knew might not be that good for me, thinking it was necessary to learn from them. Then I became aware that it was a programming that was entirely unnecessary and potentially quite dangerous. We don't need to walk dangerous paths or choose stupid things to learn what we need to know.

We have other ways to learn, much safer and more enjoyable. When we are willing to become aware, signs and symbols will assist us in learning with more grace.

We can rest easy trusting that we are constantly being guided. There are always signs. However, we often miss them because we thought these signs would look, or feel, different.

Or we don't like the one we got, so we ignore it.

Or we misinterpret it.

Ignoring—or misinterpreting—is both a habit and mis-perception. In the next chapter, we'll delve into the depths of perception. But for now, we need to recognize that no one sees anything the same. We all interpret what we experience or see from our personal, trained, educated, and accepted paradigm, or perspective.

In addition, in our belief in humanness, we have minimal and constricted views of the world. We see fewer colors than birds, smell fewer smells than dogs, notice much less than an ant.

To make it worse, we are constantly comparing, regretting, reviewing the past, and being afraid of the future.

Humans, what are we going to do about them?

Here's what we are going to do. We are going to remember that we are actually not human and forgive ourselves when we forget.

We are in Truth the essence of all that the Divine expresses, which includes all those amazing miraculous things that the natural world encompasses.

We use mirrors of all kinds to discover, uncover, and reveal the universe's true nature and of ourselves. We pay attention to signs and symbols.

But we don't want to get stuck in the sign or symbol. Signs and symbols are not anchors. They are guideposts on our path. Signs and symbols are not places to build a house or belief system to live in forever, forgetting that there is so much more.

If we believe them to be real rather than only signs and symbols, we will be locked into the accumulation of things rather than be free to be the full expressions of boundless life.

Evil acts are often committed after a sign or symbol "tells" someone they are doing the right thing. As a fiction writer, I often have the antagonist believe that the signs and symbols are aligning for them to do something evil.

We want to avoid making a sign or symbol conform to what we want to see and hear—because they will.

We interpret everything from our personal internal point of view. This is why we must be increasingly more willing to become aware of what we believe to be reality. And then consciously choose the reality that most aligns to our current highest understanding of good—which evolves as we break open old paradigms and belief systems.

We must develop the habit of always beginning anything with an intent to do the "next right thing" and base it on a foundation of Love, compassion, kindness, and harmony for all creation. That way, we will not be misled as often or recognize much faster when we have been.

Be willing to become aware of the signs and symbols surrounding you. As you do this, you might begin to notice, or strengthen your awareness, that there is a loving, intelligent force that underlies everything.

Be willing for this to be true. Look for signs and symbols that this is true.

Yes, I know that by doing so, we are building a perception, paradigm, belief system. But this one produces good for all beings. Yes, I believe this to be our true, what I call, big r Reality. And yes, I have to continually go back to being willing, becoming aware, and seeing the signs and symbols that support this Truth.

But since we know that *what we perceive to be reality magnifies*, I want to magnify this Reality, and it is so much easier to stay on this path when we walk it together.

TURNING THINGS INTO THOUGHTS

The truth is you are already what you are seeking. — Adyashanti

To interpret signs and symbols correctly, we need to learn and apply the skill of turning things back into their true nature—thoughts.

Yes, I know we often say this the other way around, turn thoughts into things. But going that direction is when things can go horribly wrong. Our thoughts and perceptions are not always, in fact, almost always, not the best ones to project into the world. We think we know what's best for us, but we don't, because we begin with our biases and assumptions about what we want.

Suppose we stop thinking of ourselves as a creator, a manifestor, a demonstrator and instead realize that we are the expression of an Intelligent, Loving Creator. We can give up the farce of trying to control everything and make things happen when we understand and accept that.

Instead, we are learning to get out of the way by willingly shifting our perception to becoming aware of the Intelligent One Creator. Understanding that signs and symbols surround us, we see Its handiwork. With this shift, we thrive abundantly in our lives.

We want to learn to discern what things are actually composed of—Mind's thoughts, God's thoughts, the Divine Mysteries' thoughts.

It's time to use my other favorite tool for becoming a perception master: Quality Word lists. If you have done them before, you know how powerful this tool is. If you haven't, you are in for a treat because turning things back into the essence of what they are—thoughts—well, it's the pathway to freedom, my friends.

How To do Quality Word Lists

An excerpt from my book *Living In Grace: The Shift To Spiritual Perception.*

Pick anything that you're thinking about or desiring to see and list its qualities. For example, let's say that you were thinking about a car. You want the idea, or quality, of transportation. So how would you like that transportation to look? You might say that its qualities include safety, effortlessness, speed, security, luxury, grace, convenience, and so on.

You have probably phrased this request as something you want or need. However, if you use the words need or want, they imply that you're lacking something. It is a statement of separation. As an expression or reflection of the Infinite One Loving Mind, how could you lack? However, when you believe you are lacking, you are.

What we perceive to be reality magnifies, so if we perceive lack, we receive lack. An unlimited Reality cannot lack; therefore, neither can you.

Since everything has already been created, we are asking ourselves to wake up to what has already been provided.

Steps to making qualities lists.

Remember, we are not interested in things here. Since things are in essence composed of qualities, we translate back into qualities the things of which we desire to become conscious.

- Step 1: Take a moment and list 8–10 qualities of something you want to "see." Use one word to express each quality. If you are using sentences, you have not come to the heart or essence of it.

- Step 2: There are two kinds of qualities lists: You can either list the qualities of the thing itself, or you can list the qualities of how you will feel when you have it.

For example, let's go back to the idea of buying a car. Your quality list for the thing—or car—might contain ideas such as red, fast, inexpensive, safe, etc.

If you choose to do a qualities list of how you will feel when you drive this car, it might read "wealthy, secure, free, joyful, etc."

If you wish, do both lists. Otherwise, do the list that makes the most sense to you. What you choose to see does not matter. It can be as important as having a home or as simple as setting the table for dinner. It is being conscious of the qualities of these "things" that make a difference.

Now that you have a quality word list, let's learn how to put them in order before learning how to use it.

How To Order Quality Word Lists

We denizens of Earth have a common vice: We take what we're offered, whether we need it or not. You can get into a lot of trouble that way. — Robert Sheckley

Once you have a list pared down to about ten Quality Words, it's time to put them into order.

Yes, they are already in order. But they are in order based on how you thought about them. We need to put the qualities in order based on how you feel about them.

Have you ever been at a place in your life where nothing happens towards what you want, no matter what you do? This is most likely because you have a quality or value block.

If we have two values that feel equal to us, our core self will be confused about which one to provide.

Remember our conversation about how state of mind overrides point of view? In the same way, what we feel overrides what we thought about as we made this list. Yes, the heart rules the intellect—the feminine guides our masculine life.

This is not how it plays out most of the time in the worldview. We can see how well that works. It doesn't.

Doing this exercise will be a guide for your actions to follow your heart's desires. It's one of the most powerful things we can do.

It's important to remember that the order your lists end up in will not be the same order that your intellectual mind put them in a while making them.

And you need someone to help you with this. You can't do it alone. But the person who helps you has to be in the same heart space that you are. If you can't find someone, let me know.

Once you find the person, both of you need to read the instructions listed below.

Once you understand the process, it becomes second nature, so take the time to let it sink in.

Quality Word lists not only work but are one of the most powerful and simple tools I know to shift lives.

Note: Don't look at your list while your partner is working with you, as this will engage brain and logic. What you want to engage are your heart and inspiration.

Your partner will ask you the following question each time:

"Which is more important to you?" and will give you two words on the list to compare.

Your partner must not give you any other verbal or physical cues. Don't listen to anything except your inner voice. Respond with the answer it tells you. Don't argue with it.

If you cannot choose one as more important than the other, your partner should ask you, "Which one can you not live without?"

PERCEPTION MASTERY

Notice that your mind tells you that if you choose one, you might not get the other. That fear comes from the point of view that there is never enough and that you don't deserve everything you want.

Since neither statement is true, notice these thoughts and move on. The truth is, once you are clear about what you desire to see, you will be able to see and receive all these qualities in a form appropriate for you at this time.

Your partner must compare each word with every word until you have an ordered list. The order will probably surprise you if you have stayed with your heart and trusted your answers.

Here is how I do this.

(Don't worry. This is a step-by-step process. Easy. Don't let worry get in the way.)

Take a sheet of paper. Draw a line down the middle. Write your partner's original quality words on the left.

>Put your finger on the first word on your partner's list. (This is so you don't lose your place.)

Ask the "which is more important" question by comparing the first word on the list to the second one. If they say the first word, move on to comparing the first word to the third word.

What if they say the second word is more important? Great. Cross it off and move it to the right side of the page.

Now compare the first word to the third word. If they say the first word is more important, move on.

What if they say the third word is more important than the first? Great. Cross it off.

But before you move it to the right side of the page, you have to find out if it is more important or less important than the word that is already over there.

So ask the "which is more important" question between those two words on the right.

Let's say the third word is more important than the second, so write it above the second word.

Go back to the left side of the list. Your finger is still on that first word. Compare it to the fourth word, and so on down the list until you have done the entire left side of the list.

If you have found more words that are more important than the first one, they will go to the right side after you compare them to that list, from the bottom up.

For example, you have two words on the right. The third word is first, and then the second. Now you have a new word. Compare it to the second. If it is more important, compare it to the third. If it is more important, put it at the top. If it isn't, it goes in the middle.

(Here's where you realize you need lots of spaces between the words on the right because you never know where the list is going.)

After you have completed comparing the first word all the way down the list on the left, you will have some crossed-out words on the left because they are now on the right in their right order.

Cross out the first word and add it at the bottom of the list on the right.

Draw a line under that list. You are finished with those words.

>Go to the list on the left. Put your finger on the first uncrossed out word. Compare it with the next uncrossed-out word below it.

Do the same thing with the words that you did before.

When you are done doing that with the new words, put a line under the list and start again on the left.

Usually, this takes two or three passes. But keep going until all the words are crossed out on the left and in order on the right.

Now you can move on to how to use your list.

How To <u>Use</u> Quality Word Lists

I know the secret of life: If you want to have loving feelings, do loving things. — Anne Lamott

Now that you have a quality word list, how do you use it? Of course, you could ignore it and hope things change. But now that you have put so much work into the list, why not make the most of it?

Here are the four simple ways to use your list. Walk your qualities through these steps and experience the world as it is—a spiritual universe.

- **1. Use the qualities as a filter.**

If something appears that you think might be what you are looking for and does not have at least the first four qualities—with the first one first and the rest following in order, it is not "it."

Think of the time you will save if you can quickly eliminate what is not right for you. For example, you discover that safety is first on your quality list for a means of transportation, and the car you are looking at has a deficient safety record, don't buy this car no matter how much you love it.

If you buy it, you will eventually be unhappy with it, and somehow you will unconsciously figure out how to get rid of it.

- **2. See the qualities everywhere.**

See the qualities in everything, not just in what you're seeking. Notice that they're always with you in many forms.

You have always had, and always will have, each quality on your list if you practice looking and expect to see it.

A quality does not have to belong to you. It can appear anywhere. All of what you see is your world. The goal is to notice that the quality you're looking for already exists everywhere, and since you can see it—it exists for you—now.

- **3. Be grateful for each quality as you see it.**

Be grateful for these qualities each time you see them, no matter where they occur. If the person you dislike most has one of these qualities, be thankful that you have seen this quality in your life.

Know that if it is "out there," it was first "within here," and therefore always available and part of your life.

- **4. Be and live these qualities yourself.**

This is the walk as one step as you walk your talk.

It's not as hard as one might think. If you wanted the quality and saw it somewhere in the world, you already possess it.

Remember, we can't see what we don't already know or imagine.

So embrace the quality, find ways to live it, and become whatever you wish to experience.

Perhaps you will discover that having the "thing" you wanted is no longer as important because you found that it already exists as thoughts—qualities.

Or perhaps you discover that you already have the "thing" you wanted. You didn't realize it because it didn't look the way you expected.

Using the four steps opens our eyes to what has always been and always will be ours. That changes everything. It's the shift to a spiritual perception.

Molly and Understanding Signs and Symbols

An error in the premise must appear in the conclusion. — Mary Baker Eddy

Molly decided to take the Perception Mastery steps at a pace that would allow her to spend more time contemplating each one. Every morning she reviewed Practical Willingness and Practical Awareness.

These two steps had forced her to pay more attention to her thought processes, and that has been both comforting and difficult. Comforting because she could see that doing those two steps was changing her perception of herself and the world. Difficult because not all the things she noticed made her feel good about herself.

But Molly understood that allowing the voice in her head to constantly criticize her and make her feel guilty was defiantly not making her happy.

Because Molly realized that allowing those negative thoughts about herself would not produce her desired results, she started using I Choose sheets to face and replace them. That meant she had a few I Choose sheets going at one time.

Molly also decided to ask herself these two questions every day:

1. What one thing are you willing to do and take action on? Why?

2. What is the one thing you thought you wanted to do and then discovered you are not willing to do it? Why?

Sometimes the answers were simple, like making a phone call she had been putting off and deciding she was unwilling to wear clothes that didn't fit anymore.

Other things were more personal. Molly found herself willing to do something her husband asked her to do that she would typically resent doing. And she discovered she was not willing to eat something she knew wasn't good for her.

The more aware Molly became about what she was willing to do and not willing to do, the more aware she became, resulting in being more willing. It was definitely a circle. The more willing, the more aware. The more aware, the more willing.

Molly was beginning to wonder what she had gotten herself into, but she kept going, grateful for every hint of progress and positive changes in her life.

Eventually, Molly decided she was ready to add in the step of Understanding Signs and Symbols. But she wasn't clear about what it meant. Did it mean that the world she saw outside was what she believed?

Yes, she knew Wayne Dyer had said, "We see what we believe," but she had put that aside, not thinking about what it meant if it were true.

Now she was ready to figure it out. Did it mean that she created what she was seeing? Or did it mean that she filtered through her point of view what she was seeing?

Reasoning that it would be impossible for her to be the creator of the ant she saw on the kitchen sink, let alone the sun in the sky, she knew she was not the creator of the world. Then it made sense that what she saw was filtered through her personal paradigm.

That's when being a perception master became a little bit more exciting for Molly. If all she had to do was bust open her paradigms, be willing to consciously choose and expect the highest understanding of good she had in each moment, and she was willing to do that.

Molly reasoned that if she interpreted all things through that perception, life would have to get better because she would see more of the good that was already present.

This is what Molly has done so far:

- She decided to be willing to be happy.

- She decided to be willing not to be willing to do things that didn't make her happy.

- She decided to be willing to become aware and be willing to consciously choose to face and replace thoughts that didn't support her highest understanding of good at each moment.

For this step, Molly started a list of all the signs she could see. This list included the obvious, like human-made signs, and the less obvious—to her—ones found within nature.

Then she began a list of things that could be symbols of something else. Along the way, she realized that signs and symbols are the same things. A stop sign is a sign to stop, but it is also a symbol of protection or safety.

The sun could symbolize unconditional love for all creations, and the ant was a symbol of diligence.

Molly decided that she'd be willing to become aware of a symbol each day and interpret it as a sign of perfection, goodness, love, and kindness and see what happened from there. She'd watch for signs that pointed her towards that path and signs that attempted to pull her off it.

Like a sign at a crossroads, everything that happened during the day could point her towards unhappiness or happiness.

If she found she was traveling down the wrong road, she was willing to change her mind and go back the other way. When she ran her choices through the filter, or perception, that "all things work together for good to them that love good," it was easier to see if the sign or symbol was pointing her down the right road, or it was a distraction.

Using an I Choose sheet that began with "I Choose to see the good already present" was eye-opening. Molly noticed how often she looked at what was not working rather than what was.

That night when her husband told her he couldn't go on the vacation she had been looking forward to because he had to work, she wanted to either yell at him for disappointing her or cry because that he didn't care about her feelings.

Instead, she paused and asked herself if she was willing to be happy, anyway. *Yes,* she mumbled to herself and then chose to see what had just happened as a sign that he was also choosing to be happy and that it wasn't personal.

That day Molly ran across a quote from Andy Rooney, and she took it as a sign to be grateful for what she had, which brought her back to happiness.

For most of life, nothing wonderful happens. If you don't enjoy getting up and working and finishing your work and sitting down to a meal with family or friends, then the chances are you're not going to be very happy. If someone bases his happiness or unhappiness on major events like a great job, huge amounts of money, a flawlessly happy marriage, or a trip to Paris, that person isn't going to be happy much of the time. If, on the other hand, happiness depends on a good breakfast, flowers in the yard, a drink or a nap, then we are more likely to live with quite a bit of happiness. — Andy Rooney

After that, Molly felt prepared to try making a Quality Word list. Since she was choosing to be happy, she asked herself what happiness felt like to her. If she was happy, how would she feel? It was harder to do than she thought it would be.

Molly thought that since happiness was a quality, it was something she understood. Didn't everyone understand what it meant to be happy? Apparently not, was her conclusion. She had words, but she didn't know if they were her words for how she would feel if she were happy or just what other people said about happiness.

Instead of rushing this list, she made notes to herself during the day when she had a moment of feeling happy. She also noticed when other people seemed happy and tried to experience what they were feeling. She even asked herself if her husband was happy. For now, she was not ready to ask him directly. It would mean she would need to share the work that she was doing for herself, and Molly worried sharing it would uproot the new seeds of understanding that she was gaining.

For Molly, this whole idea of turning something she wanted back to qualities was a revelation. And she decided to enjoy the process instead of rushing it. Molly thought that if she moved on to the next step in perception mastery, perhaps it would help her with what she was doing with her unfinished quality word list and strengthen her growing understanding.

Practical Signs And Symbols

To see ourselves as others see us is a most salutary gift. Hardly less important is the capacity to see others as they see themselves. —— Aldous Huxley

As you look for Signs and Symbols, try sinking into the awareness that there is a Loving Intelligence behind all that is both visible and invisible. Yes, "human" awareness teaches and leads us through sensations, and signs and symbols. Interpreting signs and symbols correctly will lead us back into an awareness of that Loving Intelligence.

Everything in nature speaks to this truth. Spend even a few minutes a day becoming aware of the immensity and beauty of what you see, even if it is only a glimpse of the sky and clouds through the buildings of a city.

The leaves of a single tree speak to the recurring abundance and the cycle of continuing life. A bee shows us the joy of what we might call work, but what a bee knows is living the essence of its purpose.

Even human-made signs point us back to a Loving Intelligence. Stop signs remind us we are part of a community. Guard rails tell us that someone cares about our safety.

The signs and symbols that direct our lives surround us. All we have to do is become aware of those who tell the truth and those who don't.

Tying It Together: Understanding Signs And Symbols

- What signs or symbols have you noticed using the skill you have already practiced in becoming aware?

- What did you learn from them?

Now back to the first step:
- How willing are you to make changes based on what you learned from being aware of signs and symbols?

These three steps are intertwined. From here on, you'll notice more and more that they live together. Become aware of signs and symbols and then be willing to take action based on what you have learned.

- Use an I Choose sheet on something you've discovered.

- Make a Quality Word list for something you want to experience. Like Molly, perhaps you don't finish it before the next step, but get started.

- When you have finished your Quality Wordlist list, get help to put them in order, and then follow the four steps to use them.

Here are some things the lying voice in your head might say to you:

"There are too many choices, so I can't decide."
Say no to this lie. Pick one.
"If you pick the qualities now, you might get them wrong."
Say no to this lie. No matter what you choose, you'll be right.
"There are more critical things to do."
Say no to this lie. What's more important than finding out how you really feel?
"You don't understand enough to do this."
Say no to this lie. Of course, you do. You are the expression of an Intelligent One Mind.

Okay, this list could go on and on. Maybe make a list of the lies that come to you so you'll recognize them in the future.

You can see how I Choose sheets and Quality Word lists go hand in hand. Sometimes the Quality Word list comes first. Sometimes the I Choose sheet. But be sure to use them both and notice how quickly things change for the better.

Note: Sometimes, the change doesn't feel like it's for the better. Sometimes things have to be cleaned out first. Don't worry. Keep going, and trust that it all is well.

5

STEP FOUR: PERCEPTION RULES

You'll see it when you believe it — Wayne Dyer

Now that we are becoming willing, aware, and noticing signs and symbols, we can focus on the heart of our shift—perception.

I love the double entendre of this step. Yes, Perception Rules, and yes, there are perception rules.

Think of your perception as a master algorithm. We know how algorithms work on the Internet. We search for something, and then we immediately see ads for it showing up everywhere.

What we see on the Internet is determined by the algorithm that has been deciding what we want to see, based on our previous actions and choices, and filtering out the rest.

Our lives are like that. Everything that has happened to us, from the moment we opened our eyes to the bright lights of this world, is set into an algorithm, paradigm, belief system that delivers what we see and experience and filters out the rest. It's not evil. It's just the way it is. And often, it's for our own good. But it also keeps us stuck. The algorithm doesn't change on its own. We have to shift it.

That perception rules is a law in the physical universe, and we can not overturn or negate. Perception produces reality, and *what we perceive to be reality magnifies*. That's how it works. We see what we believe. We might as well use it to our advantage and consciously choose what we believe.

Now that we know that perception rules, let's do a deep dive into what that means because, without understanding this step, we can get stuck in our past beliefs and experiences.

It's obvious, isn't it, that to shift anything in our life we have to shift what we believe? However, the first question to ask ourselves is not "how do I shift my perception," "but am I willing to do it?" This willingness step is one we have to check consistently.

The good news is that we have already begun the how of shifting. We have been willing to becoming aware of what we already believe. We continue to clarify that awareness by paying attention to the signs and symbols which mirror back to us what we believe.

Now for the critical step—consciously choosing a perception or a belief system that improves our life experience. Because once again, *what we perceive to be reality magnifies*. We see what we believe.

Shifting perception is not working at something to make it happen. Instead, it's allowing it to come into our experience.

If you have ever looked at a Magic Eye picture, you have experienced the result of letting go. I keep the book *Beyond 3D* near my computer and look at one page a day. After doing this for a long time, I already know what the picture will be. But if

I **try** to see that picture, I can't. To see it, I have to stop trying, let go, and let it reveal itself.

If we hold that point of view that we are the creators of our existence, not only will we find it impossible one day to sustain it, but we get in the way. Even if you don't believe that a loving, divine intelligence has already created everything, why not imagine that it's true and build that as a consciously chosen point of view?

Since perception produces reality, why not choose a point of view that there is a Divine Intelligence that lovingly creates and provides at all times for all of life? Why not let go and let life become joyous and easy?

However, we know by choosing any point of view doesn't mean the results are instantaneous. Actually, they are, but we rarely experience it because that dang algorithm filters the results out—most of the time. Sometimes all things align, and there is what we often call a magical event when actually it was a moment when all our perceptions of the universe's physicality dissolve and we see that all along it's been a spiritual universe.

So why doesn't this "magical event" happen all the time? Why the delay? Because there is not just one mode of perception, there are two modes: state of mind and point of view.

Our point of view is what we believe and want to be true. Point of view perception is what we intentionally or unintentionally use as the building blocks of our lives. We see and hear and experience points of view all the time. Sometimes we get angry at others' points of view and even our own.

Points of view are constantly on display. From the way the person at the store check-out treats you, your neighbor's garden, your friend's opinions, the people in the news opinions, what you say to your friends, what you say to yourself about the state of the world.

Noticing our point of view is imperative. How can we shift something if we don't know about it? Often we adopt the point of view of our parents, friends, politicians, community leaders, and influencers without noticing or deciding if that's really what we want to experience in life.

Points of view become ruts and habits if not consistently examined. Too often, we become prisoners of our beliefs.

The intention of the steps of Perception Mastery is to assist us in stepping out of our ruts by stretching our point of view into something that better aligns with the concept of an infinite Intelligence, a loving God, an abundant life.

This shift will open our self-imposed cell doors and change our lives for the better. Improving a point of view affects everyone equally and lovingly and is the work and practice of a lifetime.

And yet, there is a critical piece of perception that determines the outcome of that shift. Because we remember, there are two modes of perception, and they have to agree with each other.

If we desire a permanent change, we also have to shift our state of mind perception.

And what is a state of mind perception? State of mind refers to our emotions and feelings. It's what we feel to be true—either as a form of joy or fear.

Guess which mode of perception runs the show? You're right. It's our state of mind perception.

We can believe that abundance is the law of the universe all we want, but if our internal emotions and feelings reside in either fear or doubt that it is true, at least for us, our experience of life will more closely match that state of mind rather than our point of view.

To effectively and permanently shift our lives, it is critical to align the two modes of perceptions.

If we can get our state of mind perception into harmony with our point of view perception, we are in sync or in flow with the universe. Until our emotions and feelings—our state of mind—is the same as what we believe—our point of view—it will be hard to make changes. And if we somehow succeed, it will be difficult, and the change will not be permanent.

It's like driving with our brakes on. Or trying to switch channels on the TV when the batteries of the remote are dead.

Here's how perception works: Our point of view produces what we experience in life. We verify what we believe through our senses and then agree that what we see and experience is reality. With this agreement, our personal reality reproduces itself again and again. Every reproduction creates a stronger belief.

That experience, belief, perception produces an emotion, which becomes our state of mind. That state of mind strengthens our faith in our point of view, and the cycle continues.

We want to build a cycle of infinite possibilities, not a closed cycle of that's how it always has been.

Just because we decide that our point of view perception is that there is consistent, unbiased abundance, it won't change our experience very much until our state of mind agrees with it.

This works both ways, of course, for the "good" and the "bad." It explains why we get better and better at something, from growing gardens to making money. It also explains how we get stuck in ruts and can't get out.

So, let's make sure we strengthen what we want to experience, not the reverse.

Nothing we experience is how it really is, anyway. Everything we experience is the out-picturing of our personal highest understanding of Truth. We are seeing our point of view and calling it reality.

When our perceptions aren't in harmony, what we accomplish won't be as satisfying or as long-lasting. Remember, by doing this work, we are not making anything happen. We are getting out of the way.

The question is, how do we shift our state of mind?

First, by noticing, becoming aware of our emotions and feelings, not judging them. Just noticing. For example, when we pay our bills, our state of mind might be that abundance is life, but what if we are fearful that there won't be enough now or in the future?

Take yourself through the first three steps. Ask yourself: *Am I willing? What are my emotions about money? What are the signs and symbols that give me clues about my perception of money, wealth, abundance?*

The intent is to bring our emotions and feelings into alignment with our point of view.

We often ignore the ways we already know to shift our state of mind because we think we don't have the time. But, once we understand that state of mind drives our point of view, it's clear that it comes first.

I came home one day from a visit with a loved one feeling that all had gone well. I enjoyed every minute and thought that we had enjoyed the time together. Then I got a phone call and discovered that I had failed at providing what they wanted from their point of view. They said they never wanted to see me again.

At first, I was shocked. Then I was angry, then depressed, then sad, and then angry again. No amount of believing that Love is the governing force of the Universe was going to bring my experience into harmony.

So I chose a few ways I knew to calm my state of mind. I read a fiction book first. Reading a good book always takes me out into another world. Then I turned to a book that helped remind me about the reality I have chosen as my point of view.

Calmer, I spent a few minutes in meditation, then did some breathwork. Calmer still, I decided I needed to talk to someone who would understand what happened and give me some insight into what to do next. The person I called understood, listened, and gave me some excellent feedback. She also made me laugh, and that lightened the experience. After that, I was calm enough to go to a yoga class and thoroughly enjoyed it.

Yes, it took a few days before I was entirely in harmony again, and then I took action in that calm state by writing a note of apology. I had to wait a few days to do it because I kept wanting to explain myself since I didn't see that I had done anything wrong. But in this case, that would not have produced the outcome I desired, a return to harmony within myself about unconditional love, and hopefully provide some peace to the person who was so angry at me.

I never had to mail the letter. The person called and apologized and asked if we could start again.

Yes, I still had to work out my state of mind to let it all go, but I knew the steps to take, and it didn't take long before I felt free from the upset.

There were other things I could have done to bring my state of mind back into harmony. I could have gone for a walk, sat by a tree, worked in the garden, listened to music, done an I Choose sheet, a Quality word list... the ways to bring harmony to our state of mind are endless.

But when we think doing these things are a waste of time, we don't do them. Instead, it's where we must begin.

You Can't Solve An Illusion

The great acts of love are done by those who are habitually performing small acts of kindness. — Victor Hugo

Once in a while, it hits me. Life is simple. But then I forget and make it complicated again.

But, in those brief shining moments of clarity, I remember that what we experience is all perception. That's why life is simple. The answer to everything lies in the premise that all we have to do is shift our perception.

The problem is we forget this simple fact.

My sister sent me a math riddle that appeared freaky and impossible. I couldn't figure it out. Then I reminded myself to "Shift your perception and begin with a different premise." When I did that, the answer was obvious.

The riddle intended to confuse. It started with a logical premise and one that was easy to accept. But in that premise, there was no answer—ever—because the premise began with an error.

When I shifted my premise, the answer was immediately clear.

PERCEPTION MASTERY

The worldview is precisely like that. It begins with a premise that appears logical, a premise that we can easily accept. In fact, our five senses tell us it's true.

Within that premise, we search and search for answers. We read books, talk to friends, get counseling, let go of desires, and remind ourselves to have faith. But none of these methods provide an answer that works for long if they begin with a premise that is an illusion.

There will never, ever be a correct answer to an illusion.

When we begin with the correct premise, the answer is straightforward.

I was working on some writing that required me to copy what I had written in one document and paste it to another. I copied and pasted and saw nothing. In the past, I would have assumed that I didn't copy and paste correctly. I would have spent some time in confusion and irritation at the problem.

That time I paused. I started with the premise that I had copied and pasted correctly. I highlighted the area on the page that I had pasted into and chose black for the text. "Magically," it appeared. It was always there. I had pasted white text to a white page, so it was invisible to my eyes.

During a rescue attempt in the first Star Trek episode, "The Menagerie," the crew tries to blast through a mountain with their phasers. Nothing happens, so they keep firing away. Nothing changes. They give up and attempt many other means of rescue, none of which is successful.

Finally, Spock and Captain Kirk realize that the Talosians, the planet's inhabitants, are masters at creating illusions. After that discovery, Kirk and Spock begin again with the correct premise that their phasers work.

With no extra effort, the illusion of the untouched mountain dissolved, revealing the hole in the mountain that had been there all along.

It's that simple. The premise determines what we perceive as the outcome. What premise do we begin with when attempting to discover an answer or dissolve a problem?

If we begin with the premise that the worldview is correct and that our senses report the truth, we will never see the Truth and what is already present.

It takes a lot less work when we begin with the correct premise and let it reveal the answer than trying to make something work inside of an illusion.

The great teacher Christ Jesus has told us all, "Ye shall know the Truth, and the Truth shall make you free." Hum. Doesn't that sound like the idea if we begin with the Truth—the correct premise—that it dissolves the prison of the worldview without effort?

The effort belongs to the shift of perception. The effort in letting go of false premises. The effort belongs to giving up personal preferences and ego.

Once we make that shift, the work is over, and the provisions we need for our life stand revealed.

Of course, that shift is an ongoing process and practice. Yet, it is one with guaranteed results and so much more satisfying than chasing illusions.

Perception Is Fluid

We now know that memories are not fixed or frozen, like Proust's jars of preserves in a larder, but are transformed, disassembled, reassembled, and recategorized with every act of recollection. — Oliver Sacks

I handed Bill the information that Joe wanted. A few days later, I asked Joe if Bill had given it to him. When Joe replied that he hadn't, I said I would find it for him.

Thinking that Bill might have put the information on his desk, I turned to go into his office. However, the door to Bill's office wasn't there! It had disappeared.

Confused, I walked over to the wall where the door should have been and stared at it. Blank.

"I thought there was a door to Bill's office right here," I said to Joe.

"Nope, the office door has never been there," was his reply.

I knew I had seen the office right where that wall currently resided, but since it obviously wasn't there now, I decided to pretend that it existed but, perhaps in another realm, and somehow not in this one.

I know, I read too much science fiction, but it was more satisfying than thinking I had not seen it when I knew I had.

I knew the answer to where the office door was would reveal itself, eventually.

The mystery solved itself a few days later. Walking to a class, I turned and saw the open door to the office right where I had I thought it was.

At first, I allowed myself to pretend for a moment that I had stepped back into the realm where the office door existed.

Not so. Instead, I realized that there was another wall in front of the one where I had looked before. Yes, it was in the exact direction that I thought it was, but not in the same space.

Here's the point. Perception is fluid. It changes based on who we are, what we were thinking, what we are noticing, and what we believe is real.

Nobody sees the same thing the same way. Actually, we don't even remember things the same way we experienced them either. Perception is fluid.

And since it is, here's the critical question.

Why do we fight so hard to maintain how we think things once were, or how we want something, and people, to be?

Will power, stubbornness, decisions build on hurt feelings, divisions, wars, and sadness are all planted in perceptions that can be shifted at any moment.

I love the idea of free will. However, I think we have misinterpreted it and wasted its true power on wanting things how we want them to be instead of using it to shift our perception about every event, every idea, every concept, and every desire.

Because we have free will, we can choose our perception. We can choose one that is limited and restrained, or we can choose one that is expanded and open.

Have you read the book *Pollyanna* lately? In this book, Pollyanna chooses a perception of good about every event that comes into her experience. She is a master of shifting to a perception that brings good to everyone whose life touches hers. She sugarcoats nothing. She simply sees it differently.

How many things do we fight for that could quickly be resolved by shifting our perception about it to see the good? How many years do we waste wishing for something that we could easily have if we shifted our perception about how it will happen or how it will look?

With free will, we can choose whether we most want to be happy or if we want most to be right. With free will, we can choose to accept a dualist reality where some people win, and some lose, or we can choose, and act from, the perception that omnipresent Good is the only power.

Guess what. We get the one we choose.

This isn't about right and wrong. It's about choice, about fluid perception, about what kind of life we want to live.

There is no need to hang onto hurt feelings or painful experiences. Facing them, recognizing that the perceptions that trap us are false memories, and replacing them with a revised and more spiritually healthy perception improves everyone's life.

Seriously.

I was right about where the door was, except I was wrong about where the wall was that housed that door. Instead of arguing or even thinking I had imagined that door, I simply waited to see if it showed up again. It did.

Perception is fluid. Perception is not a creator; it simply shows us what we believe to be true.

So, why not choose a perception that omnipresent Good is all that is going on. If we do that together, we just might remove all the obstacles that keep us from seeing that Good IS all that is going on.

The two most powerful things we can do with our free will are to be willing to let Good direct our path and to set our feet on a path to action directed by the quiet voice within that is All-Good.

Do you have something better to do with your time than shift your perception, be willing to listen to the guidance of the Divine, and then take action? Didn't think so. Let's shift together; it's easier that way!

BROKEN PERCEPTIONS

Perhaps one has to be very old before one learns how to be amused rather than shocked. — Pearl S. Buck

You've heard the joke about the beautiful redhead that goes into her doctor's office and complains that everything hurts. Okay, here's the rest of the joke, and then I promise to make a point.

"Impossible!" says the doctor, "Show me."

The redhead took her finger, pushed on her left shoulder, and screamed, and then she pushed her elbow and screamed even more. She pushed her knee and screamed; likewise, she pushed her ankle and screamed. Everywhere she touched made her scream.

The doctor said, "You're not really a redhead, are you?"

"Well, no," she said, "I'm actually a blonde.'

"I thought so," the doctor said. "Your finger is broken!"

Don't you love how symbolic this joke is?

Not the "blonde" part, the "only one thing broken" part.

In our lives, we all do precisely what Miss Blonde did. We touch everything, from money to love, with a broken perception, and it all hurts. It feels as if everything is going wrong when all that needs to be "doctored" is our perception.

We can tell we have a broken finger by the pain we feel, and we can tell a broken perception in the same way.

It is not necessarily a physical pain. Although that can be a symptom, it is also emotional pain. We all have both kinds of pains sometimes.

One symptom of a broken perception is the anger that is being expressed these days throughout the world. There is anger over how others think or live, or act, or what they believe in, or even just what they look like.

In our own lives, we feel frustrated by the car in front of us. We snap at loved ones. Life feels limited, and happiness seeps out of our days.

All of this pain is because of a broken perception. If we have a broken finger, we take the time to heal it.

However, broken perceptions often remain throughout a lifetime, causing pain whenever it touches something.

We all know what an unbroken finger looks like, but what about an unbroken perception? What does it look like? With an intact finger, all its parts line up perfectly. Everything functions together as one. It works in the same way in an unbroken perception.

Let's take the unbroken perception or point of view that God, Spirit, the infinite intelligence of Mind, has Love as its base concept, essence, and principle. Most of us would agree that this is true about God. We also agree that God is omnipresent, omnipotent, omniscient, and omniaction. Therefore, all that can go on is Love.

So, where does the anger we spoke about come into play? We can see that to feel anger, we have to break away from the point of view that all is Love. We may say that it is true, but we don't experience that it is. Our state of mind perception is not in agreement with our point of view perception.

How do we fix this broken perception? Here's a simple way to do so. We face the damaged perception, uncover the lie that it is stating, and replace it with what is true. Yes, it's that simple.

Going back to our example of anger at someone with whom we disagree. We face the fact that we don't. Then we replace it with an unbroken perception. We call this technique "face and replace."

The replace part could go something like this:

"Because all I see and know is filled with Love, and a visible representation of Love, then there is no place for anything but Love in my thinking and experience. Because we are all One within this Love, there is no other person for me to be angry with. It's my misperception and I willingly give it up to experience the harmony of Love's presence."

As this unbroken perception replaces the broken one, what we experience in our world shifts. *What we perceive as reality magnifies,* so a broken perception produces a broken experience. A whole perception produces a whole experience, one without pain and judgment because there is no place for pain or judgment in infinite Love.

We can see how a broken perception touching any part of our life would be painful, and the unbroken perception of the Principle of Love in action would dissolve that pain.

Unlike broken fingers, broken perceptions are deliberately contagious.

It is essential to know this so that we stop spreading them. We'll know when our perception is whole and complete because our life experiences will be harmonious and joyful.

We will feel loved ourselves, and we will experience unconditional love for everyone else. This is undoubtedly worth the effort it takes to heal a broken perception.

Let's see what Molly is up to, and then go to some practical things for you to do.

MOLLY AND PERCEPTION RULES

Finish every day and be done with it. You have done what you could; some blunders and absurdities no doubt crept in; forget them as soon as you can. Tomorrow is a new day; you shall begin it serenely and with too high a spirit to be encumbered with your old nonsense. — Ralph Waldo Emerson

In the past, if her husband had disappointed her, Molly would have added that disappointment to her list of resentments about how life wasn't fair.

This time, she chose to put her disappointment aside. Instead, she decided to use her vacation as an opportunity to make choices every day based on what she wanted to do that would increase her happiness. Since she was off work for the week, she could design each day how she wanted it to be.

Getting to that decision was tough. Molly had many reasons why she didn't want to get over her disappointment. But when she realized she was building a prison of beliefs for herself, Molly decided she would use whatever tools she had to break out.

Molly started her prison break by walking herself through the perception mastery steps.

First, she knew she had to let go of how she had wanted their vacation to be and become willing to not be angry at her husband. That opened up the space to be willing to let each day be a discovery of things she wanted to do.

Molly also decided that she was not willing to ruin her time off with disappointments, regrets, and anger.

To do this, Molly realized she had to become more aware of what she liked and didn't like. Once she began to pay attention, she discovered that finding the answers was easier than she thought it would be.

Molly noticed her thoughts more often and acted on the impulses that moved her toward happiness. She did her best to reject the ideas that didn't move her towards joy. Sometimes the signs were clear, like her favorite movie was playing. Other times, she had to pay more attention.

Molly also decided to use the week to discover what she liked and didn't like about her job—and why. She started a list. Molly treated it as a research scientist, not taking what she wrote personally.

As the list grew, Molly added the step of Perception Rules. As she did this work, she got a clearer idea of who she was and how it fit and didn't fit the work she was doing. Molly noticed the opinions and beliefs that weren't hers but had accepted as hers. She noticed ideas she had carried forward from childhood that no longer fit the woman she had become.

Learning that her state of mind was affecting the outcome of her point of view was a revelation. If she approached every day of her work with dread, nothing was going to make it better.

Molly wrote what she wanted her point of view to be about work. Not the work she was doing now. Not her current job. The idea of work.

She stuck with her original point of view that she wanted to be happy and consciously chose this as her perspective about work.

Molly wrote: *"Work provides a way to express my unique gifts, and expressing my gifts makes me happy."*

To get her state of mind into harmony with this point of view, she made a quality word list of how she would feel if she expressed her unique gifts. She didn't worry about whether she knew what her unique gifts were. All she wanted to know was how she would feel if she understood and lived them.

When she finished, Molly asked her best friend to put her quality word list in order for her. She didn't tell her friend anything about what the list was or what she was doing. She just showed her the instructions for doing it.

When they finished, Molly had her quality words in order and was ready to use her list. Since her friend was curious about what she was doing, Molly gave her the *Perception Mastery* book and said, "If you like this, perhaps we can do it together because I'll be starting this over again once I got through it this time."

In the meantime, Molly took the top word on her list, "fulfilled," and began the practice of using it the four ways. When she asked herself, "What am I doing right now that makes me feel fulfilled," it helped her see how many things felt good to her. Even doing the housework and gardening gave her a sense of fulfillment.

Then she noticed when she didn't feel fulfilled and asked herself why. She didn't judge what she discovered. She simply noted it to herself.

Molly also carved out time, three times a day, to do something that quieted her mind. At first, she felt guilty about doing it. Then she realized that was the voice in her head trying to keep her in an old way of being. One she didn't want anymore.

Molly discovered she liked a routine she could count on, but one she could change if she felt the desire to do it differently that day. Once Molly realized that made her happy, she added it to her list of how she wanted to design her days.

Now, over halfway through the seven steps, Molly noticed the changes in herself. It hadn't been easy, but that didn't mean she wasn't enjoying herself. And she noticed little things in her life moving more in harmony. Molly didn't care if it had always been that way or not. What counted was she was experiencing it now.

Here is Molly's quality word list in order on how she would feel if she was expressing her unique gifts. It surprised her that the quality word happy was at the bottom of her list since that was what she had chosen first, but then she realized if she felt all the things on her list in order, she would be happy.

> Fulfilled
> Satisfied
> Joyous
> Grateful
> Humble
> Aware

Useful
Peaceful
Energized
Happy

Practical Perception Rules

Better keep yourself clean and bright; you are the window through which you must see the world. — George Bernard Shaw

To practice this step, why not look at something that disappoints you and find out why. It doesn't matter what you choose, because it will open a portal into many other parts of your life. It's all connected.

So whatever comes to mind, go with it, at least begin with it. This could be anything from your parents, children, friends, work, house, car, garden, or clothes. It doesn't have to be significant. It could be the chair in the living room, the way your hair looked this morning. Just pick something.

Tying It Together: Perception Rules

Here's an example of how to tie together what you have learned so far using the idea of feeling disappointed.

- Ask yourself, "Am I willing for this to not disappoint me?"

- Then, become aware of why you are or are not willing.

- Notice how you feel, the signs in your body or your

life that point out your disappointment.

- What perception, belief, has brought you to this disappointment?
- Are you willing to shift that perception?
- To what? Write it out.
- How would you feel if you were not disappointed?
- Make a quality list.
- Put that quality word list in order (don't forget you need help with this part.) (Chapter Four)
- Use it. Take the first word through all four steps. If you can do this with each word, go down the list in order. (Chapter Four)
- Notice if your state of mind agrees with this state of mind.
- Make an I Choose sheet to choose that state of mind.
- Take personal quiet time every day to bring them into harmony.

A few examples of things to do during that time: Meditate, walk alone, visit nature, conscious breathwork, study, listening, mindful reading,

Of course, you don't have to use the idea of disappointment. If another idea comes up for you, use that!

The good news is that as you, and I, and all the people joining us, make conscious shifts towards an enlightened point of view and state of mind, our perception shifts become easier and more effective.

6

STEP FIVE: CHOOSE SPIRITUAL PERCEPTION

We do not want churches because they will teach us to quarrel about God. — Chief Joseph

The practice of shifting perception is an ongoing process, but it is a joyful one—most of the time.

Noticing the story we have chosen to live within is tricky. We have to notice, but we can't get sucked into it at the same time. We need to remind ourselves that it's a rewrite of our story. Every story needs a rewrite. It's not personal.

Sometimes the best we can do at the moment is make the story better. That's not a bad thing. There is no need to feel guilt or regret at what we didn't do right or didn't know before.

Progression is the key. As we adjust, rewrite, and consciously choose, we move towards the opening of light that reveals that big r Reality is not a game or a story.

Until now, we could use all the steps we have learned to shift our lives, no matter what version of the worldview we chose. But now we have arrived at the step where we consciously choose a spiritual perception because this is where the difference truly happens.

And we are ready because we have been practicing a spiritual perception all along. However, in this step, we will actively choose to make it the foundation of our life.

What is a spiritual perception?

It is a dividing line between doing everything with the sole intent and purpose of making our physical life better, or doing it with the intent and purpose to know and live as our true spiritual nature. It's where we consciously choose to see all that we call physical as it is—spiritual—and let that perception shift our world and daily life into the Infinite.

This is not about what we each call God. Or what religion or church we belong to or tenets we hold dear. It's not about separation, making some beliefs right and some wrong. It's about a choice between seeing the world as material or seeing it as spiritual. Not divisive—unified.

Probably, if you have gotten this far in this book, you have already chosen a spiritual perception, or at least have a strong desire for it. All along, we have been making that choice. Every time we choose the highest understanding of good in each moment, we choose a spiritual perception—a spiritual point of view.

This step makes it more real. It grounds the choice into our belief systems. This is where we step up to the plate and say, "Yes, the multiverse is spiritual."

What does that mean practically and in each of our lives? Let's find out.

Of course, we must begin with the awareness that what we perceive to be reality magnifies. We know this doesn't mean we are Life's creator. It means we are reflectors and expressers.

This is a critical awareness. It means that when something good happens—we didn't create it, manifest it, pray it into existence, or demonstrate it. It was already present. We shifted our perception and our actions to allow ourselves to experience it.

Thankfully, it also means that when something terrible happens, we didn't do that either.

The funny thing is, we barely take credit for the good we do and berate ourselves for the wrong things we do. That doesn't sound to me what a loving Father-Mother-One-Creator called Love would do to us or want us to do to ourselves.

Or saying it simply, which is probably the best kind of perception to choose, "Whatever is not Good, Kind, Loving, and Harmonious is not True."

We want this to be an accurate statement. But every day is filled with what appears to be alternative facts.

Yet, what has become more apparent in every field of study is that our perception filters what we see and experience.

If I could wave a magic wand and wipe away the filter, film, veil, paradigm, and beliefs of what appears as a material world in all its inconsistency and pinging between opposites—we would see and experience only Love and Harmony.

As William Blake said, "If the doors of perception were cleansed every thing would appear to man as it is, Infinite. For man has closed himself up, till he sees all things thro' narrow chinks of his cavern."

Our perceptions are like clouds. The sun is always present. As we dissolve and shift those clouds and perceptions, the sun, the Truth, appears where it has always been.

And here's where the symbol of the sun comes in handy. We don't specifically see the sun. We see the rays of light, which have to pass through—or onto—an object to be seen.

We are those rays of light (expresser) and objects (reflector). As with all symbols, the analogy isn't entirely accurate when they remain within human perception, but they move the clouds away.

I figure the parting of the waves of the Red Sea and parting of cloud stories in the scriptures are the same attempt to tell us to shift our perception and see what is already True.

Perception does rule. And because it does in our human belief system, we need to know the rules of perception. But one day, if we get to the place of awareness of only the Divine, that rule vanishes. And even now, once in a while, the clouds of our mist-perceptions part, and we experience we are part of the Divine Loving Intelligence.

The Bible says it this way: *For now we see through a glass, darkly; but then face to face: now I know in part; but then shall I know even as also I am known.* — Corinthians 13:12 KJV

I imagine, like me, you yearn for that day. That's why this work means so much. It gives us a path to walk that parts the clouds, providing a glimpse of our true spiritual nature.

To get there, we consistently practice shifting our perception to a spiritual point of view using tools and techniques that work. We are students and practitioners of shifting our perceptions to more closely match the Truth of our being.

We are willing to. We are aware of what we have accepted as true. We use signs and symbols provided for us to understand our conscious and unconscious choices.

We know that shifting perception is the only way to change our lives permanently.

What is your point of view? Make it the best, highest, broadest, closest to the Divine, Great Mystery, One Awareness, Intelligent Love that you can in each moment.

Then practice bringing your thoughts, feelings, and actions into harmony with it. Anything that clouds your vision of your point of view, you can say no to.

In my book *Living In Grace*, I ask, "What if this is a game?" If you think that might be true in this small r reality, you might enjoy the book, *The Simulation Hypothesis* by Rizwan Virk.

However, game or no game, it does not negate that there is One Intelligence called Love. But it reminds us of the importance of perception and not "logging on" to any game that is not removing the clouds.

Doomscrolling will never take us out of the game or provide a perception that offers a life of satisfaction and joy.

Choose your side: peace and harmony or confusion and division.

Don't let the noise of the unreal world distract you from knowing the Truth of One Awareness, Divinity, Infinite Intelligence that is Love—and then acting from that Truth. This is not a passive decision. It is an active and ongoing practice.

And as we have discovered, it's easier together, since that is the truth of Creation, anyway. We are One.

That voice that claims you are not a ray of Divinity expressing Love and Creativity is lying to you. Maybe it thinks it's doing you a favor. But as we become more aware, we can thank it for helping and send it on its way. Or at least make it sit in the corner and be quiet.

Use your imagination here. Let it take you into the realm of the Infinite. Let yourself feel what that feels like. Only a moment of that sunlight of Love can shift anything to its native harmony.

Every time we choose a "better" perception, our world shifts. Let's decide not to be blind to that immediate shift. Celebrate every sign or symbol that something has changed for the better. Not just for you as a person. The world. Everyone in it. The universe. Everyone and everything in it.

We used to believe that we are within our bodies. You know we are not. Just because we rarely experience this doesn't mean it is not true. Send your imagination out into the vastness of unlimited Intelligent Love.

Let it be true that as you do that, you are no longer the being in the body, but you are the being of the Divine.

Imagine that!

THE DREAM AND THE DREAMER ARE ONE

I think 99 times and find nothing. I stop thinking, swim in silence, and the truth comes to me. — Albert Einstein

Here are three stories that tell a tale of dreams.

1. One morning, I woke up and said this to myself, "Today is the day I am going to go next door and tell our neighbor to stop letting his dog come into our carport and use it for a toilet."

Good idea, except we didn't have a carport, nor was there a dog that lived next door.

2. A Satellite Company had sent our information to a credit collection agency claiming that we had not returned their two receivers. This was despite the fact we had delivery proof and were assured that all was okay after calling at least five times (on that issue alone). They claimed we had taken the card out of one of them, so we owed the entire $150.00 for the receiver.

Having experienced these kinds of issues with them the entire time we had their service, my first reaction was anger at the injustice of the accusation and the fact that I had to defend myself against something we had not done.

3. It was just one more thing in our rental home that didn't work right. Turning the knob for the heater in the living room didn't make one bit of difference. I turned it up. It didn't get warmer. I turned it down, and it didn't get cooler. For weeks I fiddled with it and then decided I would call the landlord in the morning.

The following day, on the way to the phone to make the call, I walked past the knob and realized that I had been fiddling with the wrong knob for two weeks.

What makes it even sillier is I had already worked the correct knobs for over a month. It's just one day I forgot there were two.

What do these three stories have in common? I was dreaming.

In the first story, it is obvious it was just a dream. And like a dream, it is equally apparent that the dreamer—me—and the dream were one.

Okay, you may think, "But two of these stories weren't dreams. They really happened."

Yes, they did—but where did they happen? They happened in the human dream.

And once again, the dreamer and the dream were one. It was my state of mind perception and my point of view perception that "created" them.

In the incident with the Satellite Company, I was already caught up in a belief of injustice. Not just about the Satellite Company but "out there" in the world.

Aren't we all daily bombarded with reports of poverty, mistreatment, wars, crimes, and man's inhumanity to man?

This bombardment enforces the point of view perception that there is another power than Divine Love, and it's doing a great job of taking over.

This builds a state of mind perception of fear, doubt, and outrage. These two modes of perception perpetuate each other.

The story about the knobs illustrates what happens when we live in a state of mind and point of view perception that things don't work as they should.

When we only pay attention to what doesn't work, we become blind to what does.

Did you notice one more thing these three stories have in common? In each one, an outside force—a dog, a satellite company, a heater knob, made a mess in our life.

Seen symbolically, the dream about the dog made it clear to me it was time to say to myself, "Stop allowing negative thoughts to invade your life."

Playing in the dream of mortal human existence is sometimes pleasant. It's when the dream turns "bad" that we think that it just might be time to wake up.

Let's all wake up from the human worldview without waiting for things to turn nasty.

To do so, we must start from the point of view and state of mind perception that there is only One Divine Power, not two. To experience the truth of this statement, we must maintain this perception no matter how real the dream of a separate power appears to be.

A wrong statement, or perception, does not change the truth about Truth, and a correct perception does not create the Truth. It reveals it.

The Truth is, there is just One power, and it is Good.

It's time to wake up and live this Truth. It has to start somewhere. It might as well be you and me.

A Sample Spiritual Perception

Of course, we all can choose the spiritual perception that works for us. But, I thought I would include mine as a template. You are welcome to use it or tweak it to fit your personal preference.

From *Living In Grace: The Shift To Spiritual Perception*

When we choose the path of Spirituality, our point of view from that point forward must be that of big r Reality. There is no room for standing on both sides of the issue.

Let's be clear about what we mean by Reality. Reality is Heaven here and now. Reality is the Truth that what appears to be material is really Spiritual. Reality is One—of everything. There is no separation or duality. Reality is the reflection, the thought, and the creation of One Mind. The Reality is, there was never a separate material creation.

Much of the time, we have to argue attorney-style with our small-i (ego) so that it will step aside and yield to Truth. Here is the premise we are going to ask our small-i to agree to in order to walk the Spiritual path of Grace.

The Shift premise.

> There is a Higher Power.
> That Higher Power is Mind.
> There is only One Mind.
> That Mind is Infinite Intelligence.
> That Mind is Perfect Love.
> That Mind is the only Cause and Creator.
> That Mind is God and Its idea = I AM.

If you read the above and thought "religion," stop! It doesn't matter if you resisted this premise because it reminded you of religion, or if you loved it because it reminded you of religion. This is not a religious premise. Please don't place unlimited abundance within the codes and rules of religious belief. All religions have this premise at their core, but they have mostly strayed from it in order to maintain their reason for being.

If you resist knowing and accepting that there is a Higher Power, God, then perhaps you are not yet ready to live from an unlimited viewpoint, and it's still more comfortable for you to stay with your current life than to let go of limiting ideas. If so, That's okay. If you are willing at least to just look at the possibility, read on.

The most important part of this shift is to desire to know and act from the understanding of what is True—and what is True is all is God. We could also use the word Good since Good and God were originally the same word. Substitute the word Good for God if it helps you to avoid any preconceived notions about God. However, when I am using the word Good instead of God, it is not the good that is the opposite of evil, which is a limited and dualistic approach. Good in this context means Perfect One.

If you are ready for an unlimited viewpoint, you know and accept that there is a Higher Power, or at least you are willing to look at the possibility. You can call this Higher Power any name you wish, as long as it contains the understanding that there is only One, an Infinite Loving Intelligence. To make this point clear, I will discuss it from the standpoint that God, Higher Power, is Mind.

You can call God the One Taste, One Engineer, Love, Good, whatever registers within as True for you.

Is there a God? As a teenager, I briefly questioned this. My first taste of religion had been one where questioning was not allowed. This presented me with ideas from which I could draw no logical conclusions. It suggested that we could never understand God and were not allowed to try. It told me that I could never be good, that guilt was part of my being. I could not accept these teachings, so in tossing out the religion I also tossed out my understanding that there is a Higher Power.

This didn't last long. Simple things told me there was Something much more, in day-to-day life, guiding others and me.

It was an internal knowing. It was the blast of joy that came from seeing the clouds one day as I started down the stairs at my dorm. I glanced up and saw the sky through a skylight. It was awareness of the simple beauty of what I was looking at, and of the incredible Intelligence of what must have created it. It was the awareness that even though I thought I was painting a picture, or choreographing a dance, something higher than my human self was guiding me. I knew without question, as you do, that there is a Higher Power. There was something greater than my human self. I just didn't know how to make use of that knowledge. I wanted to know more about this Higher Power. After much reading, thinking, and listening, I understood that One Mind is the only answer.

Only an Infinite Intelligent Mind could hold the world and the infinity of being in Its thought. Could there be two minds running the world? No. Even two human minds can never agree totally on everything.

It has to be One Mind, an Infinite Intelligence.

The next step in this premise is that there is only One Cause and Creator. Since there is only One Mind, there can be just one Cause, one Creator. Since there is only One power, there is no other power to create something. This means there is nothing that we did or didn't do that could remove us from the State of Grace, or from being the reflection of One Loving Mind. We can breathe a sigh of relief! All we need to do is yield to the State of Grace to become conscious of the Truth of One.

The radical view that we'll soon begin to live from is that there is only One Mind, One Cause, One Creator, and It is Intelligent Infinite Love. This means that perfection, joy, and good are the Truth about who we are. The Truth is not some goal to achieve or someplace to go. When we make this kingdom of God—One Mind, Love—the starting point, all other needs are met. Heaven is here, at hand, and ours now, because it is Truth. We can live on Main Street and still be living in Heaven because there is only One Creation, God's, and that One is Spiritual. This is our Spiritual point of view.

Love's Promise—The Spiritual Laws of Grace.

1. *But, seek ye first the kingdom of God, and his righteousness; and all these things shall be added unto thee.* —Matthew 6:33, Bible

2. *Ask, and it shall be given you; seek, and ye shall find; knock, and it shall be opened unto you.* —Matthew 7:7, Bible

3. *And it shall come to pass, that before they call, I will answer.* —Isaiah 65:24, Bible

MOLLY AND SPIRITUAL PERCEPTION

I wanted to change the world. But I found that the only thing one can be sure of changing is oneself. —Aldous Huxley

Molly approached this step with quite a bit of trepidation. *What is spiritual perception*, she asked herself. Was it what she had learned in the church that she grew up in?

If so, Molly wasn't sure she wanted that one because it included a god that punished and destroyed. To be fair, she wasn't exactly sure if that was actually the basis of her parents' church, but the people in it seemed to think so.

Because although they claimed they based their church on love, she didn't think they believed that. She had seen too much hate and prejudice for people who had different beliefs than they did. If God was unconditional love, then where was theirs?

On the other hand, Molly realized they might not know that their point of view and state of mind didn't match. Still, she wanted no part of a perception that didn't begin with a point of view that there was only One Intelligence, and it was Love. Molly knew she didn't understand how that could be true, and her belief that it was true was as tiny as a mustard seed.

But Molly reasoned that if it were true that perception is reality, that was the reality she wanted.

To make it easy to remember, she chose One Intelligent Love as the basis of her spiritual perception. She then took the quality words "unconditional love" and practiced using them as the basis of her actions, using the four steps of using quality words as her guide.

Molly paid attention and noticed when and if she saw unconditional love and was grateful for seeing it and expanding her perception of what it looked like.

She asked herself to notice how she felt about people, places, and things. Did she have unconditional love for them? If not, why not?

Molly realized she had to look beyond the physical to discover something to love. Was she grateful for what she saw? Did it align with her spiritual perception of unconditional love? If it didn't, she decided it couldn't be true.

Since she wanted to be happy in her work, Molly asked herself to find a way to love each aspect of everything she did unconditionally. As she did so, she discovered something that felt very important to her.

She could love something but not like it and choose not to do it. She could love that her work provided income and safety, but not like that she felt stifled in it. Because she had love for herself, she could choose something that better matched her individuality.

As Molly discovered more about what she was willing to do or accept and what she was not willing to do or accept, she remained grateful for what she was finding. Even when she noticed her prejudices, both personal and directed towards others, she remained grateful for the awareness.

She did her best to have unconditional love for herself, too, reasoning that if she was going to stick with the spiritual perception of One Intelligence and It as Love, she had to include herself. She was not separate, as her ego and personality consistently claimed.

Molly found there was joy in the perception mastery practice because it was a path to walk. Even if she didn't like some of what she found, Molly knew she was dissolving beliefs that stood in her way of being happy.

She began to think of the work as a cleaning out of her mental home. It was a mess at first, but that was okay. She knew it was necessary—too much clutter, both in her thinking and in her house.

The quote by Antoine de Saint-Exupery, "He who would travel happily must travel light," became her guide. She would travel light, both mentally and physically. Letting go would become something she enjoyed instead of something she feared.

Molly decided to follow the spiritual perception that she was the expressor and reflector of One Intelligent Love, and observe how her thinking, actions, and life aligned or didn't align with that perception.

Practical Spiritual Perception

How wonderful it is that nobody need wait a single moment before starting to improve the world. — Anne Frank

It's time to choose your spiritual perception. I have given you mine, and Molly has given you hers. You are welcome to use them or tweak them to make them your own.

The vital part of this exercise is that you choose one. You can adjust what you choose as you practice using your spiritual perception as the basis of your days. Just make sure that your spiritual perception is the best one you can imagine today.

Use your own spiritual beliefs to choose the words that resonate with you. Let go of prejudices and other people's opinions and how others live their lives, and decide what is Truth for you.

Tying It Together: Spiritual Perception

- Write out your current highest understanding of your spiritual perception.

- Be willing for your spiritual perception to be true.

- Become aware of the times when you act as if you

don't believe it.

- Understand that the world shows us what we believe, which gives us the opportunity to bring our actions back to our spiritual point of view.

- Don't forget to spend the time you need to bring your state of mind into harmony with your point of view. Imagination comes in handy here. If you would like to strengthen and expand your imagination, you could try my book *Imagination Mastery*. It goes hand in hand with *Perception Mastery*.

- Use the face and replace tools of I Choose sheets and Quality Word lists to help align your point of view and state of mind.

This step of choosing a spiritual perception can feel fantastic. Allow yourself to believe.

Make your spiritual perception the best idea of life that you can imagine. As you let go of old beliefs and patterns, allow yourself to continue expanding your spiritual perception to be precisely right for you.

If you want real control, drop the illusion of control; and let life live you. It does anyway. — Bryon Katie

(If you would like a daily prompt to notice simple things about life that might shift your perception about them, I have a free daily email, only a few sentences long, called *The Daily Nudge* which you can find at becalewis.com.

7

STEP SIX: WALK AS ONE

Sometimes our light goes out, but is blown again into instant flame by an encounter with another human being. — Albert Schweitzer

What does walk-as-one mean? It could mean "walk your talk," and it certainly includes that idea, but walk as one prompts us to ask ourselves, what one?

It includes:
- Walk as one with our chosen spiritual perception.

- Walk as one with our state of mind and point of view.

- Walk as one with the Divine.

- Walk as one with our community, our family, ourselves.

Walk as one begins with listening to the wise, still small voice within—often called intuition or gut feelings—and then taking the action it suggests and encourages us to do.

Walk as one is living as our unique spiritual blessings and sharing them with others.

This step often gets overlooked or given lip service but is not actually taken. It can be the step where we get stuck because we aren't living our spiritual point of view. Talking about it, maybe. But not living it.

Putting our point of view and state of mind into appropriate action "proves" that we believe what we say. It's a practice. But we don't need special equipment, or special times in the day to practice. The opportunity is always present.

Walk as one is about relationships. All relationships. The relationship with ourselves and with other people, places, and things. It's about what we want for ourselves and what we wish for others. Walk as one is considering how our actions affect others.

When we walk as one, we acknowledge our kinship with all living things.

Walk as one always contains action. Always.

When we walk as one, we take action to provide what others need when we can. When we see something wrong, we speak up. Without action, all that we believe in is only words. Pretty words sometimes, but useless without helpful action.

Talking about kindness and doing nothing kind or nothing to stop unkindness is worse than useless.

The Bible tells us this, "For as the body without the spirit is dead, so faith without works is dead also." — James 2:26

It also tells us we can know the tree by the fruit it produces. No amount of lovely words makes up for treating others with contempt or disrespect. That tree is rotten, no matter how beautiful it looks on the outside.

When our actions do not match our point of view or state of mind, we fool ourselves. And it's important to remember that some people hold a point of view and state of mind that is not about harmony, love, community, unselfishness, and kindness. They have chosen the opposite. And some of them are incredibly proficient at speaking words that mislead. Pay attention.

Liars and pretty words have fooled us all at one time or another. It's a dangerous resemblance and often hard to detect. I found release from one such person when I became fully aware of how they made me feel and how they separated me from my loved ones, and the expression of myself. I had noticed the fruit of the tree.

Ask yourself, "What is their intent? Do they advocate walking as one? What one? Is it about the unity and equality of all things?"

Try not to get lost in the "how" of all of this. I don't have the answers. I don't think anyone does. There are more things that we don't know than what we do.

But you and I do know that perception produces reality, and because of that, we choose the best reality we can imagine.

Do I make mistakes? Absolutely. I can get lost in criticism, resentment, self-pity, discouragement, anger, too. But as I practice, I notice more quickly when I have fallen off the path, and I am grateful for the tools and support around me that help me get back on.

Walk as one is the opposite of the belief that we can attract what we want by thinking about it with no action required. It would be lovely if this were true. Or would it?

Everyone would stay home expecting the thing they want to show up at their door. There would be no community or sharing of gifts. There would be no proof that our faith is genuine.

Not taking action on what the still small voice leads us to do is faith without works. And it is a waste of the unique gifts and talents we have been given that are meant to support, encourage, and inspire others within our chosen community. Without action, we are robbed of the joy of working and learning together. Yes, action is always required.

But it is not about how significant the action is that we take. Every step, no matter how small, is equally important. Each of us does what our gifts and talents enable us to do. Walk as one is a tapestry of threads, each one necessary for the fabric of lives to be complete.

Most of the time, we don't know the impact of our actions. But if we intend to bless and support others in their life, then we don't need to worry if it worked out okay.

We only have to watch the cycle of nature to see that Life is reciprocal. We give and we receive. But often, it is not a direct response. When we go to the store, hand the clerk money, we immediately receive what we paid for.

But Life is often not that direct, nor should we expect it to be so. Life is more of a cycle, a spiral. But it always spins back to us. Sometimes we miss what we have received because our point of view might be that what we do never works, or people don't take care of us, or... well, this list could go on and on, and I cover this point more thoroughly in the book *The Four Essential Questions*.

In truth, Life returns to us much more than we give because It is Love loving Itself after all. What a fantastic point of view to adopt and practice bringing our state of mind into harmony with it. Imagine how much good you and I would accept in our life if we were fully walking as one. Knowing and living that point of view, we would never hoard what we receive. We'd let it go, knowing there is always more.

In this Earth game, we must overcome the belief of lack and at the same time be in harmonious and balanced relationships.

There is nothing we can do, think, or say that is not about a relationship. Truth is practical; therefore, our expression of Truth will be practical and useful.

When we apply and use the Truth in every relationship we have, including our bodies, supply, work, and loved ones—we walk as one.

How glorious is that?

Is Spirit Calling Your Name?

Attitude follows action far more often than action follows attitude. We change our mood as a result of how we act. If you want to feel a certain way, begin by acting as if you do. On the other hand, if you truly want to accomplish something, waiting for the mood to strike is ineffective. — Seth Godin

We were at the local corn fest and had arrived just in time to hear the raffle announcer say, "Coleen Springer, you have won the bike."

It was a cute little bike. I am sure Coleen would have loved it. They kept calling her name, and when she didn't answer, they said they would draw again.

So, Coleen, or a parent, spent the time and money to purchase a raffle ticket, had hoped she would win the bike, and yet they were not present for the drawing.

Do we do the same? Do we practice, study the science and spirit of God, and yet decide to take time off, hoping we won't miss our name being called?

Yes, that's what we do. We get distracted by the out-picture we call our lives. The claims that it is more fun to do something else mislead us. Or the lie that we have studied enough.

Moments go by, days go by, years go by, and how often has our name been called without our knowing it? Called for gifts of the heart. Called to pick up the supplies we asked for. Called to do a good deed, called to stop danger, or called to correct the illusion that danger has occurred.

There are other ways we can miss Spirit's calling other than being not present. One way is to ignore it. We do that all the time, too.

Once, while out jogging, I heard my name being called and actually did what it requested for me to do.

You are probably thinking, "Oh my, how glorious, it must have been something very important."

No, it wasn't. In fact, Spirit's calling is almost always about being faithful to the small details of life, and when we prove we are present and listening, we hear the message more often, clearer, and yes, sometimes it is something "important" to do.

In this case, it was something very simple. I was jogging in the early dawn and saw a clump of marigolds lying in the road. Something or someone had pulled them out of the garden.

I heard the voice, "Replant them."

I ignore it and kept running. I heard the voice again, "Replant them."

That time I turned around, grabbed the flowers, found the hole they came out of, replanted them, said a few words of encouragement to them, and then continued down the road. It took less than a minute to do this.

It is very doubtful anyone saw me, and the homeowner probably never knew what I had done. Yet, I am the one who benefited. I saw those flowers every time I jogged by, happily growing as if it never happened. Most of all, I benefited because I heard the call and I answered it.

Spirit is calling with these messages: "Stop following the lies of the worldview. Don't be afraid; follow my voice. Hold hands with your neighbor and walk this way. Do good without expectation of return. Be diligent, stay in Truth, don't get distracted. The time is now, not later."

The consequences of not being present are far more serious than not receiving the bike meant for you. It is a dangerous decision to take time off from living the whole truth of God at all times or to ignore the voice of Spirit that is calling you.

The reward is much greater than a bike. Yes, it is work, but there is no other work as worth doing. It is the experience of heaven on earth now. It is the awareness of grace in your life now. It is the awakening to your true spiritual nature, the Am in I Am.

Your name is always being called. Be sure you are prepared and present to hear and act on it.

MOLLY AND WALK AS ONE

You get treated in life the way you teach people to treat you. — Wayne Dyer

One day, Molly ran across something written fifty years ago by Oldham and Hackman about the characteristics of work that produced satisfaction and fulfillment. The five questions meshed perfectly with the practice she was doing using the four steps of quality words with her list of how she would feel if she was fulfilled in her work.

She found an article by *Seth Godin* that broke the article down into five factors:

1. Task significance: Does the work you do create meaning or impact?

2. Task identity: Do you feel ownership (emotionally) in the work you're doing?

3. Autonomy: Do you have the freedom to make choices?

4. Skill variety: Is the task monotonous?

5. Feedback: Are you in a place where you can safely and easily get feedback and use it to improve?

The answer for Molly was no to every question except the question, "is the task monotonous?"

Yes, her work was boring. But not only at work, but the work she did at home. However, now that she had become more aware that her beliefs played a significant role in how she experienced life, Molly wondered if it was her job and home life's fault or how she approached it?

So she went back to the steps of perception mastery.

She asked herself if she was willing to do work that created meaning and impact. Molly realized it was partially the work, but mostly her feelings about it that made it feel unimportant. Washing dishes didn't create meaning or impact unless she used it to express her gift of order.

Molly asked herself to be more aware of how her attitude affected her work, the people she worked with, and, of course, her husband. If she was always unhappy, how did she make others feel?

By paying attention to the reactions of others to her presence and what they said to her helped her recognize the signs and symbols all around her.

Molly reminded herself of the perception rule that *what she perceived as reality magnified*. Could she change her perception, her point of view and state of mind, about work and her husband?

Yes, she decided. She was willing to choose a spiritually based perception for her work, husband, and other relationships.

Which meant she had to act as if it were true. *Geez,* she muttered to herself, *that might be the hard part.* But, once again, Molly was willing.

All week her husband had been going to work while she stayed home. At first, it had been hard to let go of the resentment that he had not taken her on the vacation she had wanted. But as the days wore on, and she followed the perception mastery steps, without even noticing it, her resentment had faded away.

It was then that Molly realized she had begun to walk as one with her point of view and state of mind. Yes, it was only baby steps, but it was making a difference in how she felt about herself, her work, her husband, and the other people in her life.

And that night, when her husband helped her with the dishes instead of heading off to do his own thing, she said "thank you" and meant it. Instead of letting resentment fester beneath the surface, she faced it and replaced it with how she wanted to feel.

Molly took her list of quality words and wrote a sentence with them. Molly didn't worry about the order, only about her intent to walk as one with her point of view and state of mind.

Writing the quality words this way helped her remember what was important to her, so she memorized her sentence and repeated it as an affirmation to herself as often as possible during the day.

Molly's sentence:

"Expressing gratitude brings fulfillment, happiness, and peace. Being useful, I am energized, satisfied, and joyous. When I am aware, I am humbled by the presence of Love."

Practical Walk As One

A learning experience is one of those things that says, "You know that thing you just did? Don't do that." — Douglas Adams

You've learned many practical ways to walk as one. All that remains is doing them.

It doesn't matter how big an issue you face or how small, you can walk it through these steps.

Tying It Together: Walk As One

Want to change your hairstyle? Thinking about moving? Need a new idea for a book you're writing? Does a relationship need to be addressed? The seven steps can go quickly or take days, weeks, or even months.

However, sometimes the first step gives you the answer you seek.

"Am I willing to change my hairstyle?" You ask yourself.

"No," you answer. Done. That's it.

However, if you want to know why you don't want to change your hairstyle because you know it would probably be a good idea, the next step would be to become aware of why you are unwilling.

Ask yourself: *What is my perception about this? Is my state of mind in harmony with my point of view?*

One way to begin is to do an I Choose sheet.

Write something like this, "I want a new hairstyle."
Check Chapter Three to remind yourself how to complete this. It may surprise you that the reasons behind this unwillingness carry into multiple areas of your life.

Perhaps, in the end, you remain unwilling, but you will know why you are unwilling, which makes all the difference. Doing the I Choose sheet helped you become aware while removing old beliefs and providing clarity.

The other tool you could use here is a Quality Word list. How would you feel if you had a new hairstyle?

Once you have them in order, take the first word through the four ways to use a list. Then go down the list one word at a time. You can review the steps in Chapter Four, but here's the synopsis.

1. As a filter.

2. As an awareness and signs and symbols check.

3. As a gratitude practice.

4. As a walk as one practice—as you live as those qualities yourself.

It doesn't matter how big or small the question you are asking is, or the item you are working with. A new dining room table or a significant business transaction may seem miles apart. But they are all connected. And it is always about relationships—with ourselves and the people, places, and things that make up our experience of the world.

- Remember to stop at least once a day and pause in silence without an agenda. Be aware of the noise, but let it go. Listen within, with no expectations, desires, wants, or needs.

- Once you have walked yourself through these steps, write a sentence with all your quality words and use it as an affirmation. Not about something you want, but a statement of fact.

I know you can guess the last step; we've already included it in this step. But there is always more to learn about gratitude, isn't there? Ready to be grateful? Let's go do it!

Where there is love there is life. — Mahatma Gandhi

8

STEP SEVEN: CELEBRATE WITH GRATITUDE

In the external scheme of things, shining moments are as brief as the twinkling of an eye, yet such twinklings are what eternity is made of—moments when we human beings can say, "I love you," "I'm proud of you," "I forgive you," "I'm grateful for you." That's what eternity is made of: invisible imperishable good stuff. — Fred Rogers

Celebrate with gratitude is an interesting play on words. Because we would think that if we were celebrating, we were grateful, or if we are grateful, we are celebrating.

But that's not always the case.

Many celebrations have nothing to do with gratitude. And sometimes we feel grateful and aren't happy about it. Yes, everyone knows the value of feeling grateful, but how often do we consciously practice, sinking deep into the feeling and not the words?

To truly celebrate with gratitude, we have to be paying attention. Of course, that's what we have been doing all along—paying attention—and then shifting the story to a better one.

It seems simple enough. And it is. The idea of it is simple. It's the execution of it that takes practice—having a system for that practice. Thankfully, we have one, the seven steps of Perception Mastery.

Here's how we walked those steps:

First, we chose to be willing.
Then we chose to become aware of what we, consciously and unconsciously, were thinking and doing.
To help us become more willing and aware, we paid attention to signs and symbols and interpreted them correctly—to the best of our current ability.
Then we began to study and understand how perception rules. We diligently adjusted our perceptions to match what we want to experience. Not just for ourselves, but for others, too.
In this book, we have walked the path of spiritual perception together. We have increased our willingness to shift, listen, and take action based on the point of view that there is an Infinite power and that One power is Love in action.
With all that in place, it was easy to walk our talk. Well, maybe not easy. But easier to be willing to do it.
It has become easier to walk away from anything that doesn't bless ourselves and others. Easier to choose to always begin with the still small voice within ourselves.
We have learned how to—and continue in—the correct identification of ourselves. We have practiced ways to silence any voices and ideas that debase who we are or someone else is.

Why? Because we know that voice lies. That's its nature, not ours.

So, of course, we are willing to celebrate because we have a proven path to walk on and dependable people to walk with us.

And we are aware that Love loving Itself is the Reality we want to live within. And we know how to dispel any illusion saying otherwise. Or at least we know it can be done—and we are willing to do it.

We celebrate with gratitude that there is a path to follow.

We celebrate with gratitude that like-minded souls walk that path with us, making it safe and comfortable.

We celebrate that the process is the point. That Life isn't about competition—it's about cooperation. We celebrate that we know that Life is not about how much stuff we acquire. It's about living as our true spiritual essence.

We celebrate because we know that we have never left the Truth of harmony. We celebrate because we know our path is to shift our perceptions to see what is already and has always been present. We celebrate because we are opening our hearts and minds to enable ourselves to see.

As we walk the ever-expanding circle of our increasing awareness, we celebrate with gratitude—for what we now know, understand, and have put into practice.

Our gratitude is unending for the awareness that as we shift to spiritual perception and focus on our highest understanding of an infinite unconditional Love, what is untrue is revealed. We are grateful that we know all untruths can be dissolved by facing and replacing them with the point of view and state of mind that we are all One within Divine Love.

We remind ourselves that the purpose of becoming perception masters is not to change the outside picture but to know and experience and be the activity of Infinite Intelligent Love.

We are grateful that in doing so, what appears as an outside picture will shift to reveal that what we need and want is already present.

You Can Rewrite The Stories Of Your Life

Before you speak, let your words pass through three gates: Is it true? Is it necessary? Is it kind? – Rumi

Core values, family history, worldview agreements, and personal habits all come together to produce a movie we call our life.

If these ideas come together to form a pretty picture, then life is good; when they don't, then life is not so good. In the not-so-good times, we stand in the middle of this movie, like characters on the screen, and try to change it.

We try to adjust the picture on the screen, forgetting it is a projection. We forget that the movie and the movie viewer are one. It is a projection of our point of view and belief systems.

This is not a whimsical idea. This is a fact.

In the book *Biocentrism* we read, "Moreover, if one accepts that the external world occurs only in Mind, in consciousness, and that it's the interior of one's brain that's cognized 'out there' at this moment, then, of course, everything is connected with everything else."

PERCEPTION MASTERY

This means it is absolutely possible to change our lives. Why? Because our lives are the out-picturing (but not the creation) of what we believe and perceive to be true.

It also means that there is only one way to make a change: to shift our perception from within.

But what if we want more than just a better life? What if we want to be what we really are? What if we want to experience ourselves as the outcome or idea of the infinite Mind or omnipotent Light? What then?

To do this, we must re-think reality and reset our perception. We must stop identifying ourselves as human. We must stop believing what the five senses tell us and listen instead to the quiet voice within.

We stop acting as if the movie and script are real. We stop wanting the story to get better and want instead to let go and live as the idea of God.

This is a radical thought and decision. It demands a root change. It follows the biblical word "repent," which means turn around and walk the other way.

We turn away from the movie playing in our heads, which results in what we call our lives.

We turn away from identifying ourselves as human and reset our thinking and perception.

It demands that we let go of how we want it to be, think it is, and then follow through with action and commitment to Truth.

This radical shift demands that we turn away from trying to fix things and people. We turn away from our story. Instead, we turn to the fact that what exists in our lives, and who we think we are, is one and the same, and be grateful for this spiritual fact.

This is not a halfway decision. It is a complete shift. Yes, it may appear to take time to reset habits and beliefs, but that too is only set within our agreement of what is true.

It may appear that others need to change first. Again, not true. What appears as they, or that, is really our own perception. There is no way to separate the thinker from what it is thinking.

Our responsibility is not to create, control, or make happen. Our responsibility is to stop separating ourselves from the ever-present infinite intelligent flow or force we call God.

Our responsibility is to let go and be what we are, which in turn resets what we experience as our lives.

As we do this, we can expect more beauty, peace, abundance, grace, happiness, love. We can expect all the fruits of good to be more present in and as our lives.

Not because we worked at becoming good and wise humans, but because we gave up the story.

We consistently listen and follow the still, small voice within. We pay attention to the symbols that prove the presence of God. We continually reset our perceptions to match our current, highest, and best understanding of the Divine.

And then, because we have refocused the projector, the movie we call our life must conform.

This surely is something to celebrate with gratitude.

Let's check on Molly one last time and see how she is doing with these seven steps and the practice of gratitude. And then onto a review in the Practical Gratitude section.

MOLLY AND GRATITUDE

The most important things in life aren't things. — Anthony J. D'Angelo

We are not the same persons this year as last; nor are those we love. It is a happy chance if we, changing, continue to love a changed person. — William Somerset Maugham

Molly believed that this step would be the easiest of all of them. After all, who doesn't know how to be grateful?

Apparently not her. To Molly's dismay, she discovered she wasn't willing to be grateful for many things. Resentment and anger simmered just below the surface about so many things that gratitude was not something she wanted to feel. After all, she had a right to those feelings, didn't she?

Molly decided she did. So she sat down in her favorite chair with a pen and paper and followed the Perception Mastery steps to let herself be angry and resentful. She was willing, aware, and saw all the signs that pointed to why she was right to feel that way.

Then she got to perception rules. That's where things fell apart.

Molly had begun to understand that her perception was "creating" her outside world, revealing to her precisely what she wanted to see. Her beliefs and perceptions filtered through everything to support the story she told about her life. She wrote the story and continued to support it by not facing and replacing it as needed.

If she wanted to experience the world through the perception that it was unfair, hard, unloving, and full of work she didn't like to do and people she didn't want to see, then that was what she would get.

The question was, would that make her happy and fulfilled? If it did, then she could continue with that same perception. But Molly knew it wouldn't.

Begrudgingly, Molly moved onto the next step, choosing a spiritual perception. She stuck with the one she had been working with, *One Intelligence and It is unconditional Love* because Molly didn't think she was in the right frame of mind to make up another one.

That meant she was back to the last step, celebrating with gratitude.

No, she was still not wholly willing to be grateful. She could feel herself clinging to the story she had been telling herself about life, but Molly decided she could be grateful that she was now aware of what she was doing. She could be grateful that the choice was hers to make. She could be grateful to herself for getting started on this fresh path.

It surprised Molly to discover that letting in just those few drops of gratitude started melting away her resentment. It was still there, so she turned her attention to being grateful for simple things, like the sunrise, the wind in the trees, her favorite ice cream in the freezer.

The more she practiced being grateful, the easier it became, and Molly was grateful, knowing that eventually her anger and resentment would fade away. But in the meantime, she wouldn't be mad at herself for having those feelings.

By the end of Molly's week off, she realized she was looking forward to going back to work. She made a list for herself of why she was happy about it. Some things on the list surprised her. Others didn't. She still wasn't sure she wanted to stay at that job, but Molly knew she would know what to do next as she practiced the seven steps.

The anger at her husband because of their ruined vacation plans had dissolved without her even noticing. Instead, she found herself thanking him for what he did that made her happy. Although he still did things she resented, they had become less important to her. It was a small step, but it made her happy to be grateful rather than angry.

Although only a few weeks had gone by since Molly had begun this practice, she could feel and see the difference in how she was experiencing life. There was a sense of relief in her heart when she fully realized that what she could change was herself. And how to change herself was to shift her perception and that she knew she could do.

People are like stained glass windows: they sparkle and shine when the sun is out, but when the darkness sets in, their true beauty is revealed only if there is a light within. — Elisabeth Kubler-Ross

Practical Gratitude

It does not do to dwell on dreams and forget to live. — J. K. Rowling

You realize that our mistrust of the future makes it hard to give up the past. — Chuck Palahniuk

Dear reader, you made it!

Doing these seven steps was like one of those outdoor circuit training paths, wasn't it? You know the ones: Stop here and do a pull-up. Stop here for lunges.

The Perception Mastery path stopped for willingness, awareness, noticing signs and symbols, understanding perception rules, choosing a spiritual reality, walking as one, and gratitude.

We are stronger, more flexible, and more joyful for taking this trip around the circuit and will become more so as we go around the path over and over again. Unlike the paths stuck on the one plane of the dimension called the Earth Game—this path spirals up and out into infinite possibilities.

You have tools to use along this path. Now that you have arrived at gratitude, why not do another I Choose sheet about something you want to expand or be grateful for?

Then perhaps make a Quality Word list of how you would feel if you were always in gratitude. Once they are in order (remember you can't do this yourself, you need someone outside you to ask the questions). Go back to Chapter Three to remind yourself how to do that and then go to Chapter Four to review the four steps for using these quality words.

Yes, you'll end up in gratitude again since it is part of step two. Gratitude is always part of any path to happiness.

- Write a sentence using those quality words, and let it help guide you into that perception, both as a point of view and a state of mind. Say it in front of a mirror. Go ahead. Do it.

Remember that *what we perceive to be reality magnifies.*

Or we could say it this way:

- The multiverse is composed of infinite possibilities.

- We narrow down the Infinite Possibilities by what we observe.

- What we observe is what we believe to be true.

- Changing our perception and beliefs changes what we observe, which then reveals a different possibility.

Every day, we have multiple opportunities to shift our perceptions. Remember, there are infinite possibilities, so there is no point in getting stuck in a perception that does not serve you, the ones you love, or the world.

We can choose to let life get better. We can choose to perceive life as good, harmonious, and abundant for everyone all the time. Yes, that means we are constantly shifting our perceptions. But why not do it? No matter how wonderful life is now, we are just getting started with the possibilities of expressing our unique spiritual gifts.

Keep up your practice. Go back through the book. It's always here for you. Make use of it!

Life is a celebration of Itself. We have joined together in that celebration, and I am profoundly grateful for you. Each person walking this path makes it easier for all of us. Thank you!

There are only four questions of value in life, Don Octavio. What is sacred? Of what is the spirit made? What is worth living for, and what is worth dying for? The answer to each is the same: only love. — Don Juan

Author Notes

I hope you found this book useful. I know these seven steps work—if we use them. Sometimes even I forget. I'll find myself in some kind of crisis, or confusion, and then remember that I have steps to take to get myself out of them.

This path—the seven steps to shift—is the first path I designed while teaching my first Shift Class in 1992, and I, and countless others, have used them since. I know they work.

So don't let them sit unattended in this book. Practice them. Let these steps help shift your life to the one you want to experience. That's the point of this shift series of books, after all—to make a difference.

Every shift of perception towards the point of view that we are all part of one glorious Loving Intelligent One moves us closer to that day when we see clearly who we, and all beings, are in Truth.

Thank you again for walking this path with me. If you feel moved to, please share this book and perhaps write an honest review so others can decide if this is for them. A few sentences is all it takes.

And, if you like this book, you might like other books in The Shift Series. You can find them on my website at becalewis.com, and everywhere you buy and read books, including your library. Look for the free book section on my website!

Remember to get your free workbook for this book at perceptionu.com.

Thank you for reading, and shifting with me, Beca

ACKNOWLEDGMENTS

I could never write a book without the help of my friends and my book community. Thank you, Jet Tucker and Jamie Lewis for taking the time to do the final reader proof. You can't imagine how much I appreciate having you in my life.

Thank you to every other member of my Book Community who helps me make so many decisions that help the book be the best book possible.

Thank you to all the people who tell me that they love to read these stories. Those random comments from friends and strangers are more valuable than gold.

And as always, thank you to my beloved husband, Del, for being my daily sounding board, for putting up with all my questions, my constant need to make things better, and for being the love of my life, in more than just this one lifetime.

ABOUT BECA

Beca writes books she hopes will change people's perceptions of themselves and the world, and open possibilities to things and ideas that are waiting to be seen and experienced.

At sixteen, Beca founded her own dance studio. Later, she received a Master's Degree in Dance in Choreography from UCLA and founded the Harbinger Dance Theatre, a multimedia dance company, while continuing to run her dance school. After graduating—to better support her three children—Beca switched to the sales field, where she worked as an employee and independent contractor to many industries, excelling in each while perfecting and teaching her Shift® system, and writing books.

She joined the financial industry and became an Associate Vice President of Investments at a major stock brokerage firm, and was a licensed Certified Financial Planner for over twenty years. This diversity, along with a variety of life challenges, helped fuel the desire to share what she's learned by writing and speaking, hoping it will make a difference in other people's lives.

Beca grew up in State College, PA, with the dream of becoming a dancer and then a writer. She carried that dream forward as she fulfilled a childhood wish by moving to Southern California in 1968. Beca told her family she would never move back to the cold.

After living there for thirty-two years, she met her husband Delbert Lee Piper, Sr., at a retreat in Virginia, and everything changed. They decided to find a place they could call their own, which sent them off traveling around the United States. They lived and worked in a few different places before returning to live in the cold once again near Del's family in a small town in Northeast Ohio, not too far from State College.

When not working and teaching together, they love to visit and play with their combined family of eight children and five grandchildren, read, study, do yoga or taiji, feed birds, and work in their garden.

ALSO BY BECA

The Rivers of Time Series: Women's Lit, Friendship, Small Town, Mystery, Magical Realism, Small Town Fiction
The Returning, The Awakening, The Rising

Follow Me Here: **Women's Lit, Friendship, Small Town, Mystery, Magical Realism, Small Town Fiction**

The Ruby Sisters Series: Women's Lit, Friendship, Mystery, Small Town Fiction
A Last Gift, After All This Time, And Then She Remembered, As If It Was Real, Almost Innocent

Stories From Doveland: Women's Lit, Friendship, Small Town, Mystery, Magical Realism, Small Town Fiction
Karass, Pragma, Jatismar, Exousia, Stemma, Paragnosis, In-Between, Missing, Out Of Nowhere

The Return To Erda Series: Fantasy
Shatterskin, Deadsweep, Abbadon, The Experiment

The Chronicles of Thamon: Fantasy
Banished, Betrayed, Discovered, Wren's Story

The Shift Series: Spiritual Self-Help
Living in Grace: The Shift to Spiritual Perception
The Daily Shift: Daily Lessons From Love To Money
The 4 Essential Questions: Choosing Spiritually Healthy Habits
The 28 Day Shift To Wealth: A Daily Prosperity Plan
The Intent Course: Say Yes To What Moves You
Imagination Mastery: A Workbook For Shifting Your Reality
Right Thinking: A Thoughtful System for Healing
Perception Mastery: Seven Steps To Lasting Change
Blooming Your Life: How To Experience Consistent Happiness

Perception Parables: Very short stories
Love's Silent Sweet Secret: A Fable About Love
Golden Chains And Silver Cords: A Fable About Letting Go

Advice / Journals
A Woman's ABC's of Life: Lessons in Love, Life, and Career from Those Who Learned The Hard Way
The Daily Nudge(s): So When Did You First Notice

www.ingramcontent.com/pod-product-compliance
Lightning Source LLC
Chambersburg PA
CBHW070908080526
44589CB00013B/1216